WEALTHY APPETITE:
FIRST THE PEOPLE AND MONEY WILL FOLLOW

ONESIMUS MALATJI

Copyright © 2023 ONESIMUS MALATJI
All rights reserved.

Wealthy Appetite: First the People and Money Will Follow
By: Onesimus Malatji

Copyright ©2023 by Onesimus Malatji
Cover Design by CiX Connect
Interior Design by CiX Connect

Trademark Notice:

All trademarks mentioned within this book belong to their respective owners.

All rights reserved. No part of this publication may be reproduced, distributed, or transmitted in any form or by any means, including photocopying, recording, or other electronic or mechanical methods, without the prior written permission of the publisher, except in the case of brief quotations embodied in critical reviews and certain other non-commercial uses permitted by copyright law.

For permissions requests, contact the publisher at:
ony@cixconnect.co.za

Copyright Violation Warning:
Unauthorized reproduction or distribution of copyrighted material is against the law. Any unauthorized copying, distribution, or use of material from this book may result in legal action.
Fair Use Notice: This book may contain copyrighted material used for educational and illustrative purposes. Such material is used under the "fair use" provisions of copyright law.

Disclaimer:
The information provided in this book is for general informational purposes only. The author and publisher are not offering legal, financial, or professional advice. Readers are advised to consult appropriate professionals for advice specific to their individual situations.
Accuracy Disclaimer: While every effort has been made to ensure the accuracy of the information presented in this book, the author and publisher cannot be held responsible for any errors, omissions, or inaccuracies.

Fair Use Notice: This book may contain copyrighted material used for educational and illustrative purposes. Such material is used under the "fair use" provisions of copyright law.

Third-Party Content:

This book may reference or include content from third-party sources. The author and publisher do not endorse or take responsibility for the accuracy or content of such third-party material.

Endorsements:

Any endorsement, testimonial, or representation contained in this book reflects the author's personal views and opinions. It does not imply an endorsement by any third party.
Results Disclaimer: The success stories and examples mentioned in this book are not guarantees of individual success. Actual results may vary based on various factors, including effort and circumstances.

Results Disclaimer:

The success stories and examples mentioned in this book are not guarantees of individual success. Actual results may vary based on various factors, including effort and circumstances.
No Guarantee of Outcome: The strategies, techniques, and advice provided in this book are based on the author's experiences and research. However, there is no guarantee that following these strategies will lead to a specific outcome or result.

Fair Use Notice:

This book may contain copyrighted material used for educational and illustrative purposes. Such material is used under the "fair use" provisions of copyright law.

DEDICATION

Being one of the difficulties in my family, always stubborn, I thank God I turned out alright. I dedicate this book to my mother, Esther Malatji. I will always love you. You have raised me well until I became a fully grown man. Thank you for your prayers and support during my tough times in life. Additionally, I extend my heartfelt dedication to my family, Thank you. I love you so much.

ACKNOWLEDGMENTS

I extend my deepest gratitude to everyone who has been a part of this incredible journey, both seen and unseen. Your support, encouragement, and unwavering belief in me have been the driving force behind the creation of this book.

To my family, for standing by me through thick and thin, for believing in my dreams, and for being a constant source of inspiration – your love and encouragement have been my guiding light.

To my friends, mentors, and colleagues, your valuable insights and feedback have shaped the ideas within these pages. Your willingness to share your wisdom and experiences has enriched this work beyond measure.

To all those who have supported me on my path, whether through a kind word, a helping hand, or a moment of shared understanding, thank you. Your presence in my life has made all the difference.

To the countless individuals who have faced challenges and setbacks, yet continued to strive for greatness, your stories have fuelled the inspiration behind these words. May you find solace and encouragement within these pages.

And finally, to the readers who have embarked on this journey with me, thank you for allowing me to share my thoughts and experiences. It is my hope that this book serves as a beacon of hope, a source of guidance, and a reminder that fulfilment can be found in every step of life's intricate tapestry.

With heartfelt appreciation,

Onesimus Malatji

WEALTHY APPETITE:
FIRST THE PEOPLE AND MONEY WILL FOLLOW

TABLE OF CONTECT	PAGES
1. Dreams in Apartheid	8-13
2. The Birth of a Visionary	14-18
3. Barriers of Race and Ambition	19-23
4. Crafting the Revolutionary Software	24-28
5. The Hard Decision: Selling to the USA	29-33
6. From Tech to Turf: The Soccer Venture	34-38
7. Uplifting the Township Team	39-43
8. A Community's Beacon of Hope	44-48
9. The Rise to Prominence	49-53
10. Jealousy Among the Elites	54-58
11. Conspiracy Shadows	59-63
12. The Bank Scandal Unfolds	64-68
13. Caught in a Web of Deceit	69-73
14. Public Fall from Grace	74-78
15. Asset Confiscation: The Takedown	79-83
16. The Darkness of Despair	84-88
17. A Prisoner of Injustice	89-93
18. Liberation and Loss	94-98
19. Rebirth Under a New Name	99-103
20. Quiet Steps to Recovery	104-108
21. Rebuilding in the Shadows	109-113
22. The Dawn of Democracy	114-118
23. Navigating a New South Africa	119-123
24. A New Era for Business	124-130
25. Unseen Influence	131-135
26. The Legacy Continues	136-140
27. Secrets of Success	141-145
28. Empowering the Next Generation	146-150
29. Soccer Team's International Glory	151-155
30. A Community Transformed	156-163
31. Revelation of the Past	164-168
32. Facing Old Demons	169-173
33. Truth and Reconciliation	174-178
34. Mending Broken Bridges	179-183
35. A Vision Realized	184-188
36. The Power of Unity	189-193
37. Final Redemption	194-198
38. Legacy of a Leader	199-202
39. Epilogue: First the People, Then the Money will follow	203-205
40. Afterword	206-208

WEALTHY APPETITE:
FIRST THE PEOPLE AND MONEY WILL FOLLOW

DREAMS IN APARTHEID

In the heart of a bustling South African township, nestled amidst the vibrant chaos and the relentless pulse of daily survival, Thabo Mokoena stood as a beacon of silent rebellion. The township, a labyrinth of narrow alleys and makeshift homes, was alive with the spirit of its inhabitants, yet shadowed by the oppressive hand of apartheid. Here, in this cradle of hardship and hope, Thabo's story began.

Thabo, with his keen eyes and a mind that raced far ahead of his years, was an anomaly in the township. His family, like many others, was a tapestry of resilience woven through generations of struggle. His father, a stern yet loving man, worked tirelessly in a local factory, while his mother's laughter often echoed in their modest home, a soothing balm against the harshness of their reality.

From a young age, Thabo exhibited an insatiable curiosity for the world beyond the confines of the township. He was particularly fascinated by the burgeoning field of technology. Radio broadcasts, rare glimpses of television, and discarded electronic parts – these were the puzzle pieces that ignited Thabo's imagination. In his hands, they transformed into dreams of innovation and progress.

But the dreamer's path was strewn with thorns. Thabo's aspirations clashed with the brutal truths of apartheid.

In school, he learned quickly that his ambitions were deemed too lofty for someone of his race. His teachers, bound by the same chains of prejudice, often dismissed his questions, stifling his thirst for knowledge.

Yet, Thabo refused to let his spirit be crushed. Each night, under the dim light of a single bulb, he sketched ideas and wrote down his visions. He saw potential in every challenge, solutions where others saw dead ends. His dream was clear - to pioneer in a field where few dared to tread.

His family's reactions to his ambitions were a mix of awe and worry. His mother's eyes sparkled with pride, yet she feared the world would not let her son soar. His father, more pragmatic, warned Thabo of the dangers of aiming too high. "Dream, but remember the ground beneath your feet," he would say.

As Thabo stands at the precipice of adulthood, his dreams undimmed by the harsh daylight of reality, the township, with its unyielding spirit and complex tales, had sown in him the seeds of determination. Thabo Mokoena was ready to embark on a journey that would challenge the very foundations of the world he knew.

The streets of the township, always bustling with life, became Thabo's classroom. He observed the comings and goings, the small businesses struggling to thrive under restrictive laws, and the community that rallied together despite everything. It was in these streets that Thabo's resolve solidified. He would not only succeed for himself but also for his community, to show that even in the face of great adversity, greatness could emerge.

His evenings were spent in fervent study and experimentation. Thabo turned a small corner of their family home into a makeshift workshop, where old radios and computers, gifted by sympathetic individuals who recognized his talent, were dismantled and reassembled. Each component told a story, each circuit held a lesson. His parents, though initially bewildered by his peculiar hobby, grew to respect his dedication.

The narrative then shifts to a pivotal moment in Thabo's life. A local entrepreneur, Mr. Khumalo, who owned a small electronics repair shop, noticed Thabo's potential. He offered him an apprenticeship, providing Thabo with his first real opportunity to delve into the world of technology. Under Mr. Khumalo's guidance, Thabo's skills flourished. He was a natural, understanding complex concepts with ease and bringing innovative solutions to common problems.

However, Thabo's journey was not without its setbacks. The harsh realities of apartheid meant that his opportunities were severely limited. He was often reminded that in South Africa, a black man's ambitions needed to be tempered with caution. Thabo grappled with these limitations, torn between his desire to push boundaries and the need to stay safe in a society that was hostile to people like him.

In these early years, Thabo also experienced first-hand the brutalities of apartheid. He witnessed friends and neighbours harassed and brutalized by the authorities. These incidents left an indelible mark on him, fuelling his determination to succeed against all odds. He began to understand that his struggle was not just for personal success, but also a fight against a system designed to keep him and others like him down.

The chapter concludes with Thabo, now a young adult, standing at a crossroads. He had the skills, the knowledge, and the ambition. But the path ahead was fraught with challenges unknown. With the unwavering support of his family and the mentorship of Mr. Khumalo, Thabo was poised to take his first steps into a world that was not ready for him. But he was determined to make it ready, to carve out a space for himself and for those who would follow.

This first chapter sets the foundation for Thabo's journey, illustrating his early life and the influences that shaped his character. It shows a young man with extraordinary talent and vision, growing up in a world that was simultaneously full of potential and fraught with peril.

THE BIRTH OF A VISIONARY

In the burgeoning glow of the African sun, as it cast long shadows across the vibrant township, Thabo Mokoena's journey continued. This chapter, "The Birth of a Visionary," delves deeper into the events and experiences that shaped Thabo into a budding entrepreneur and a symbol of hope for his community.

The chapter opens with Thabo's family history, painting a vivid picture of the generations that preceded him. His grandparents, who had lived through the early days of apartheid, instilled in their family a sense of resilience and the importance of education. Thabo's parents inherited this legacy, striving to provide their children with opportunities they never had. This historical backdrop provides a deeper understanding of the values and motivations that drive Thabo.

As a child, Thabo exhibited an extraordinary intellect and an unquenchable thirst for knowledge. He was not just bright; he was innovative, often coming up with solutions to everyday problems that amazed his family and neighbours. His mother fondly recalled stories of Thabo fixing broken household items or inventing simple gadgets to ease their daily chores.

School, for Thabo, was a double-edged sword. It was a place of learning and discovery, but also a space where the limitations imposed by apartheid were most palpable.

Despite excelling academically, he often felt stifled and misunderstood by his teachers, who were either indifferent or unable to nurture his burgeoning talents. Yet, these challenges only served to fuel his determination.

The narrative then shifts to a significant turning point in Thabo's life. A chance encounter with a discarded computer, thrown away by a wealthy family, became a pivotal moment for him. With a mixture of curiosity and reverence, Thabo brought the computer home, spending countless hours learning to repair and operate it. This computer was not just a machine; it was a window to a world of possibilities, a glimpse into a future that Thabo yearned to be a part of.

Thabo's passion for technology soon became an obsession. He devoured books, magazines, and any material he could find on electronics and computing. He began to dream of creating technological solutions that would not only elevate his own circumstances but also those of his community and, perhaps, his country.

The chapter also explores Thabo's early entrepreneurial ventures. He started by repairing radios and televisions in his neighbourhood, quickly gaining a reputation as a young prodigy. These small ventures were not just about making money; they were exercises in learning and innovation, stepping stones towards bigger aspirations.

As Thabo grew older, his vision began to take a more definite shape. He didn't just want to be a technician; he wanted to be an innovator, a leader in the field of technology. He dreamed of building a company that would break the moulds of apartheid, a beacon of African innovation and excellence.

"The Birth of a Visionary" concludes with Thabo, now a teenager, gazing up at the starlit African sky, pondering his future. The challenges ahead were immense, but so were his ambition and resolve. Thabo Mokoena was not just dreaming of a better future; he was preparing to create it.

This chapter builds upon the foundations laid in the first chapter, further developing Thabo's character and setting the stage for his future endeavours. It showcases his early achievements and the formation of his visionary goals, highlighting the internal and external forces that shaped his path.

As Thabo gazed at the stars, he reflected on the stories his grandfather used to tell him. Stories of a South Africa where everyone had equal opportunities, stories that seemed like distant dreams in the current world. These tales, imbued with hope and resilience, echoed in Thabo's mind, weaving into his dreams of changing the world through technology.

Thabo's early teenage years were marked by a deepening understanding of the world's complexities and injustices. He began to grasp the broader implications of apartheid, not just as a political system but as a barrier to innovation and progress. He realized that his journey was not only about personal success but also about breaking barriers for his community.

His resolve was tested time and again. Limited resources, lack of access to advanced technology, and the scepticism of those around him were constant challenges. But Thabo's resourcefulness knew no bounds. He started to innovate with whatever materials he could find, creating makeshift gadgets and devices that amazed and inspired his peers.

One of Thabo's most significant projects during this time was a small solar-powered radio, which he built using salvaged parts. This radio became a symbol of hope and ingenuity in the township, a testament to what could be achieved with limited resources and unlimited imagination.

Thabo's journey was not a solitary one. He found allies and mentors along the way. One such mentor was Mrs. Jacobs, a retired school teacher who recognized Thabo's potential. She provided him with books and encouraged him to think critically about the world. Her guidance helped Thabo to hone not only his technical skills but also his leadership and entrepreneurial abilities.

As Thabo entered late adolescence, his aspirations began to crystallize into a more defined vision. He wanted to establish a technology company that would not only be a hub of innovation but also a training ground for young, aspiring black South Africans who were, like him, constrained by the limitations of apartheid.

The chapter ends with Thabo organizing a small community event, where he showcased his inventions and shared his vision for the future. The event, though small in scale, was a significant moment for Thabo. It was his first step towards becoming a leader in his community, an advocate for change through technology and innovation.

"The Birth of a Visionary" is a chapter of growth and realization. It portrays Thabo's evolution from a curious child into a determined young adult with a clear vision for his future. His journey symbolizes the potential of the human spirit to overcome adversity and the power of dreams to drive change.

BARRIERS OF RACE AND AMBITION

Barriers of Race and Ambition, delves into the heart of Thabo Mokoena's struggle as he confronts the systemic racism and societal limitations that threaten to stifle his burgeoning dreams. It is a poignant exploration of the challenges he faces as a black entrepreneur in apartheid-era South Africa.

The chapter opens with Thabo, now in his late teens, increasingly aware of the stark inequalities that pervade every aspect of life in South Africa. His ambitions, which once seemed boundless, begin to collide with the harsh realities of an unjust system. This collision brings a sense of frustration, but also a fierce determination to overcome these obstacles.

Thabo's efforts to take his small technology ventures to the next level are met with a series of rejections and roadblocks. He applies for loans and pitches his ideas to potential investors, only to be turned away because of his race. These experiences are disheartening, but they also serve to highlight the deep-seated prejudices and systemic barriers that black South Africans face.

The narrative then shifts to a defining moment in Thabo's life. He attends a technology expo in Johannesburg, a rare opportunity to immerse himself in the latest advancements and to network with industry professionals.

However, his excitement quickly turns to disillusionment as he faces overt racism and exclusion. Despite having innovative ideas and a clear vision, Thabo finds himself marginalized and ignored.

This experience at the expo proves to be a turning point for Thabo. He realizes that the conventional paths to success are largely closed to him, and that if he wants to succeed, he will have to forge his own path. This realization is both daunting and galvanizing. It forces Thabo to think creatively about how to circumvent the barriers in his way.

Thabo's resilience in the face of these challenges inspires those around him. His family, friends, and even sceptics in the community begin to see him not just as a dreamer, but as a beacon of hope in a society riddled with inequality. Thabo starts to mentor and teach other young people in the township, sharing his knowledge and skills, and in doing so, sowing the seeds for a future generation of black entrepreneurs.

As the chapter concludes, Thabo makes a pivotal decision. He resolves to start his own company, no matter how small or challenging the beginnings might be. He begins to gather a team of like-minded individuals, pooling their resources and skills. This decision marks the birth of not just a business, but a movement – one that challenges the status quo and paves the way for change.

"Barriers of Race and Ambition" is a testament to Thabo's unwavering spirit and his refusal to be defined or defeated by the circumstances of his birth. It sets the stage for his journey into entrepreneurship, against the backdrop of a society grappling with deep-rooted racial injustices.

As Thabo embarks on this new venture, the challenges he faces become more complex and daunting. He and his team begin working out of a small, makeshift office in the township. They have limited resources, but what they lack in materials, they make up for in passion and ingenuity. The team consists of young, talented individuals from the community, each bringing their own unique skills and perspectives.

The stark contrast between their humble setup and the high-tech world they aspire to enter does not deter them. Instead, it fuels their creativity. They start by tackling small projects, leveraging Thabo's knowledge of electronics and the team's collective resourcefulness. They repair and refurbish old computers, develop basic software solutions for local businesses, and even begin experimenting with their own innovations.

However, the external barriers are only part of the struggle. Internally, Thabo grapples with the weight of his ambitions. He feels a deep responsibility towards his team and the community. His dream has grown beyond personal success; it has become a collective mission to break the cycle of poverty and disenfranchisement.

Thabo's leadership is put to the test as they face numerous setbacks. Their work is often met with scepticism, not only from the white-dominated industry but also within their own community, where some view their efforts as futile against the towering might of apartheid. Thabo, though shaken, remains undeterred. He becomes a source of strength and inspiration for his team, encouraging them to persevere.

The chapter takes a turn when Thabo's team manages to create a basic but functional software program designed to help small businesses manage their finances. This small triumph is a significant milestone for the team. It proves to themselves and to the community that they are capable of producing valuable, marketable technology.

Their success, however, does not go unnoticed. They begin to attract the attention of both potential allies and adversaries. Some local business owners express interest in their software, while certain figures in the established tech industry view them as a threat. This attention brings new challenges, as Thabo and his team must navigate a landscape riddled with hostility and exploitation.

As the chapter closes, Thabo reflects on the journey so far. The physical barriers of race and ambition are daunting, but the psychological barriers are equally challenging. The doubts, fears, and insecurities that come with trying to achieve the seemingly impossible.

Yet, in the faces of his team, in their small victories and unwavering determination, Thabo sees a glimmer of the future he is fighting for.

"Barriers of Race and Ambition" is a chapter of conflict and triumph, highlighting the internal and external struggles that Thabo and his team face as they strive to make their mark in a world that seems stacked against them. It is a story of resilience, unity, and the relentless pursuit of a dream.

CRAFTING THE REVOLUTIONARY SOFTWARE

Crafting the Revolutionary Software, delves into the heart of Thabo Mokoena's technological journey, marking a pivotal phase in his quest to break barriers and redefine possibilities. This chapter captures the essence of innovation, determination, and the spirit of overcoming adversity.

The chapter begins with Thabo and his team celebrating their small success with the business management software. Buoyed by this achievement, Thabo sets his sights higher. He envisions creating a software solution that could revolutionize the way businesses operate in South Africa, especially for those in underprivileged communities like his.

The team, now more cohesive and driven, starts brainstorming ideas. They identify key challenges faced by local businesses: lack of access to technology, inefficient processes, and limited market reach. Thabo proposes developing a software that not only addresses these issues but also is user-friendly for those not well-versed in technology.

The narrative then shifts to the gruelling process of developing this software. The team works tirelessly, often late into the night, in their cramped workspace. They face numerous challenges: limited resources, intermittent electricity, and outdated equipment. However, these limitations spur their creativity.

They devise ingenious solutions, repurposing old hardware and writing efficient code to make the most of their limited computing power.

A significant part of the chapter is dedicated to a breakthrough moment. After months of relentless work, the team finally develops a prototype. It's a simple yet powerful tool that integrates various business functions—inventory management, financial tracking, and customer relations—into a single, user-friendly platform. This prototype is more than just a piece of software; it's a symbol of hope and a testament to what can be achieved against all odds.

Thabo's leadership and vision are central to this chapter. He not only guides the technical development of the software but also fosters a sense of purpose and camaraderie among his team. His ability to inspire and motivate becomes a driving force behind their progress.

As they prepare to test the software in a real-world environment, Thabo faces a new set of challenges. Convincing local business owners to try their product is difficult. Many are sceptical, hesitant to trust a new technology, especially one developed in a township. Thabo's persistence and the tangible benefits of the software gradually win them over.

The chapter reaches a crescendo when a local grocery store agrees to implement their software. The successful deployment of the software in this store leads to immediate improvements in efficiency and profitability. Word begins to spread, and soon other businesses express interest.

However, this success does not go unnoticed by the powers that be. The established tech industry, dominated by large corporations, begins to view Thabo's team as a potential threat. This attention brings new challenges and risks, setting the stage for future conflicts.

"Crafting the Revolutionary Software" is a chapter of triumph over adversity. It showcases Thabo's journey from a dreamer in a township to an innovator making tangible changes in his community. The chapter ends with Thabo and his team standing at the cusp of something great, unaware of the challenges and opportunities that lie ahead.

The success of their software in the local grocery store marked a turning point for Thabo and his team. Emboldened by this achievement, they began to refine and enhance their software, adding features and improving user-friendliness. The software, which started as a basic tool, evolved into a robust platform capable of competing with offerings from established tech companies.

The narrative shifts to focus on the impact of the software on the local community. Small business owners, who were initially sceptical, started to see tangible benefits. They experienced increased efficiency, better inventory management, and improved customer relations. This success story spread quickly through the township, and soon, Thabo's team was inundated with requests from other businesses eager to utilize their technology.

Thabo, realizing the potential of their creation, started to dream bigger. He envisioned their software not just as a tool for local businesses but as a product that could be scaled and used nationwide, perhaps even internationally. This ambition, however, was not without its challenges.

The chapter highlights the team's efforts to scale their operation. They needed more resources, better equipment, and access to broader markets. Thabo started reaching out to potential investors, pitching his vision of a tech company that could bridge the gap between advanced technology and the needs of underprivileged communities.

Their efforts, however, were met with mixed reactions. While some investors were intrigued by the potential of the software and Thabo's passion, others were hesitant to invest in a company based in a township, led by a young black entrepreneur. The legacy of apartheid still loomed large, casting a shadow of doubt and prejudice over their endeavours.

Despite these setbacks, Thabo remained undeterred. He believed in the power of their software and the talent of his team. The chapter delves into Thabo's growth as a leader, showcasing his ability to navigate these complex challenges while keeping his team motivated and focused.

As the chapter nears its conclusion, a breakthrough occurs. Thabo secures a meeting with a group of international investors who are interested in technology solutions for emerging markets. The meeting is tense, filled with hard questions and scepticism, but Thabo's eloquence, combined with a demonstration of their software, impresses the investors.

The chapter ends on a hopeful note. The investors agree to fund Thabo's venture, providing the resources needed to scale their software and bring it to a wider market. This success is a significant milestone for Thabo and his team, a validation of their hard work and a testament to the power of innovation and resilience.

"Crafting the Revolutionary Software" is a narrative of growth, perseverance, and the breaking of boundaries. It is a story about how a small team from a township, armed with talent and determination, managed to create something that challenged the status quo and opened doors to new possibilities.

THE HARD DECISION: SELLING TO THE USA

The Hard Decision: Selling to the USA, narrates a critical juncture in Thabo Mokoena's journey, where he faces a dilemma that tests his values, ambitions, and the very essence of his entrepreneurial spirit. This chapter is a deep exploration of the complexities and challenges that come with success and growth.

Following the investment from international backers, Thabo and his team begin scaling their software for a larger market. The chapter opens with a whirlwind of activity: upgrading their facilities, hiring more staff, and refining their product. The team is energized, and their software quickly starts gaining traction not only in South Africa but also in other African countries.

However, with this rapid expansion comes increased scrutiny. Thabo's software, once a local innovation, is now on the radar of major global tech companies. These corporations, recognizing the potential of Thabo's software to disrupt the market, begin to show interest. Among them is a large tech firm from the USA, which extends an offer to buy Thabo's company.

Thabo is torn. On one hand, this offer is a validation of all the hard work and sacrifices made by him and his team. It's an opportunity to secure his and his team's future financially and to bring their software to a global stage.

On the other hand, selling to the U.S. company feels like a betrayal of his original vision — to uplift his community and country through local innovation.

The narrative delves into Thabo's internal conflict. He consults with his team, his mentors, and his family. Each conversation brings different perspectives. His team is divided; some see the sale as a golden opportunity, while others fear losing the essence of what they've built. His mentor, Mr. Khumalo, advises him to consider the long-term impact of his decision on the community. His family, ever supportive, urges him to follow his heart.

Thabo also grapples with the realities of the tech industry and the limitations of operating in a market still influenced by racial and economic disparities. Selling to the U.S. firm would mean more resources and a broader platform, but it could also mean losing control over the direction and soul of their software.

The chapter reaches its climax when Thabo, after much deliberation, decides to accept the offer from the U.S. company. This decision is not made lightly; it comes with a heavy heart and a deep sense of responsibility. Thabo negotiates terms that ensure his team remains integral to the software's future development and secures commitments for investment in local tech initiatives.

As the chapter concludes, Thabo reflects on the journey that led him to this point. He realizes that this decision, though difficult, opens up new possibilities. It's not the end of his dream but a transformation of it. He sees it as a chance to impact the tech industry on a global scale and to bring the lessons and successes from his journey to a wider audience.

"The Hard Decision: Selling to the USA" is a poignant chapter that encapsulates the complexities of success, the weight of responsibility, and the challenging decisions that define an entrepreneur's journey. It portrays Thabo's growth as a leader and a visionary, capable of making tough choices for the greater good.

In the aftermath of the sale, Thabo and his team face a period of profound change. The once small, tight-knit group is now part of a large, international corporation. This transition brings with it a mix of excitement and apprehension. While the infusion of resources and the expansion of their platform is exhilarating, there is an underlying fear of losing their identity and the core values that drove their initial success.

The narrative explores the integration process, highlighting the cultural and operational challenges that arise. Thabo, who once led his team with autonomy and a shared vision, now finds himself navigating corporate structures and politics.

He works diligently to protect his team's interests and to ensure that their voices are heard in the larger organization.

As Thabo adjusts to his new role, he also grapples with feelings of guilt and doubt. He wonders if he has compromised his ideals for financial gain and questions the impact of his decision on the community that inspired and supported him. These feelings are intensified by the reactions from the township, where some view his decision as a sell-out, while others see it as a step towards greater achievements.

Amidst these challenges, Thabo begins to see the positive outcomes of his decision. The software, now with global reach, is having a significant impact. It's being used to empower small businesses in various countries, creating opportunities and driving economic growth. Furthermore, the U.S. company honours its commitment to invest in local tech initiatives, leading to the establishment of new educational and training programs in Thabo's community.

Thabo's personal growth is a central theme in this chapter. He comes to understand that his journey is not defined by a single decision but by his ability to adapt and maintain his values in changing circumstances. He realizes that his influence has expanded, allowing him to advocate for diversity and inclusivity in the tech industry on a global stage.

The chapter concludes with Thabo returning to his township, where he is greeted with a mix of scepticism and admiration. He organizes a community meeting to share his experiences and to outline his future plans, which include setting up a foundation to support local entrepreneurs. As he speaks, Thabo feels a renewed connection with his roots and a clear vision for his future path.

"The Hard Decision: Selling to the USA" is a chapter of transition, portraying the complexities of success and the nuances of growth and change. It illustrates Thabo's resilience and his commitment to staying true to his values, even as his world expands beyond the boundaries of the township. The chapter ends with a sense of hope and anticipation for what Thabo will achieve next, both for himself and for his community.

FROM TECH TO TURF: THE SOCCER VENTURE

From Tech to Turf: The Soccer Venture, marks a significant shift in Thabo Mokoena's entrepreneurial journey. After navigating the complex world of technology and innovation, Thabo turns his attention to a new passion project: transforming a local soccer team into a beacon of hope and success in his community.

The chapter begins with Thabo reflecting on his childhood in the township, where soccer was more than just a game. It was a unifying force, a source of joy and community spirit. This nostalgia, coupled with his desire to give back to the community that raised him, inspires Thabo to invest in a struggling local soccer team.

Thabo's approach to the soccer venture is infused with the same innovative spirit he brought to his tech endeavours. He starts by investing in the basics: upgrading the team's equipment, improving their training facilities, and hiring experienced coaches. His goal is not just to build a winning team, but to create an environment where young talent can be nurtured and developed.

The narrative delves into the challenges Thabo faces in this new venture. The world of sports, especially in a township setting, comes with its own set of complexities. Thabo encounters scepticism from those who question his motives and his ability to make a difference in the soccer arena, a field far removed from his tech background.

Despite these challenges, Thabo's passion and commitment begin to pay off. The team, which once struggled to attract players and supporters, starts to show signs of improvement. Their performance in local leagues improves dramatically, drawing attention and support from the wider community.

Thabo's involvement in soccer extends beyond the field. He recognizes the sport's potential to impact the community positively. He organizes youth development programs, using soccer as a tool to engage young people and keep them away from the pitfalls of township life, such as crime and substance abuse.

The chapter also explores the personal satisfaction Thabo finds in the soccer venture. The joy and pride evident in the players and the community provide him with a sense of fulfilment that differs from his achievements in the tech industry. Soccer brings a more immediate and tangible impact, visibly uplifting the spirits of the players and supporters alike.

As the chapter progresses, the soccer team starts to gain regional recognition. Their success stories attract media attention, shining a light on the positive changes happening in the township. Thabo's vision of using soccer as a platform for community development is becoming a reality.

The chapter concludes with the team winning a crucial regional tournament, a victory that symbolizes much more than a sporting triumph. It represents the culmination of Thabo's efforts to empower and uplift his community. This victory is a testament to the power of vision, passion, and perseverance in creating positive change.

"From Tech to Turf: The Soccer Venture" is a chapter about transformation and impact. It illustrates Thabo's ability to channel his success into meaningful community engagement, showcasing the multifaceted nature of his entrepreneurial spirit. The chapter ends with Thabo looking on proudly as the team celebrates, a reminder of the potential that lies in every corner of the township, waiting to be ignited.

As the euphoria of the regional tournament victory settles, Thabo's vision for the soccer team begins to expand. He starts to see the team not just as a symbol of athletic success but as a platform for broader community development and empowerment. This perspective shift marks the beginning of a new chapter in Thabo's journey, one that intertwines sports, community upliftment, and social entrepreneurship.

The narrative then shifts to Thabo's strategic planning for the soccer team's future. He begins by strengthening the team's infrastructure. This includes not only improving training facilities and equipment but also focusing on the players' education and well-being.

Thabo introduces academic tutoring for younger players and life skills training for the team, ensuring they have opportunities both on and off the field.

Thabo also leverages his business acumen to secure sponsorships and partnerships for the team. He pitches the soccer team as a brand that represents resilience, hope, and community spirit. His efforts attract local businesses and even some international brands, bringing in much-needed funds and raising the team's profile.

The team's growing success on the field mirrors Thabo's efforts off it. They start climbing the ranks in national leagues, drawing larger crowds and media attention. The players, many of whom came from humble beginnings, become local heroes and role models for the township's youth.

However, with increased visibility comes new challenges. Thabo and the team face pressure to maintain their performance and to represent their community positively. Additionally, the attention from media and sponsors brings a level of scrutiny that the team is not accustomed to. Thabo navigates these challenges with a careful balance of professional management and personal touch, always keeping the team's and community's best interests at heart.

A significant portion of the chapter is dedicated to a landmark event organized by Thabo – a community soccer festival. This event brings together teams from various townships, creating a platform for young talent to showcase their skills. The festival is more than a sporting event; it's a celebration of culture, unity, and the power of sports to transcend social barriers.

Thabo's soccer venture also begins to influence other aspects of community life. The team's success instils a sense of pride and optimism in the township, sparking initiatives in other areas such as education, arts, and entrepreneurship. Thabo uses his influence and resources to support these initiatives, reinforcing his commitment to holistic community development.

The chapter concludes with a reflective Thabo watching a sunset over the township, contemplating the journey so far. He realizes that the soccer venture has become a conduit for his larger vision of empowering his community. The success and challenges he has faced reinforce his belief in the potential of sports as a tool for social change.

"From Tech to Turf: The Soccer Venture" is a story of growth, impact, and the intertwining of dreams and reality. It highlights Thabo's ability to transform his success into a catalyst for community upliftment, using the universal language of soccer to inspire, unite, and empower. The chapter ends with a sense of anticipation for what this venture will achieve next, both for Thabo and for the community he holds dear.

UPLIFTING THE TOWNSHIP TEAM

Uplifting the Township Team, zooms in on Thabo Mokoena's efforts to transform the local soccer team into a source of pride and inspiration for the entire township. This chapter highlights the power of sports as a unifying force and its role in fostering community spirit and hope.

The chapter begins with the team basking in the glory of their recent successes. However, Thabo understands that the team's impact can extend far beyond the soccer field. He envisions the team as a catalyst for positive change in the township, a symbol of what can be achieved with hard work, unity, and dedication.

Thabo's first step is to improve the team's facilities. He invests in renovating the playing field, equipping it with better lighting and seating to accommodate more spectators. He also upgrades the training equipment and provides the team with professional-grade gear. These improvements are not just about enhancing performance; they're about instilling a sense of dignity and self-worth in the players.

The narrative then delves into Thabo's efforts to engage the team with the community. He organizes soccer clinics for the youth, were team players coach and mentor young aspirants. These clinics are about more than teaching soccer skills; they are platforms for instilling discipline, teamwork, and ambition in the township's youth.

Thabo also recognizes the importance of education and personal development. He sets up scholarship programs for the players, enabling them to pursue academic interests alongside their soccer careers. This initiative reflects Thabo's belief in the holistic development of individuals, preparing them for life beyond soccer.

The chapter highlights a key event organized by the team - a charity match to raise funds for local schools. The event is a resounding success, drawing large crowds and media attention. It's a festive occasion, with local music, food stalls, and exhibitions, turning it into a celebration of the township's culture and spirit.

Amidst these developments, the soccer team continues to excel in their league, drawing attention from national sports organizations. The players become role models in the community, their stories of perseverance and success resonating with the township's youth.

However, Thabo's efforts are not without challenges. He faces resistance from some community members who question his intentions and the commercialization of the team. Thabo navigates these concerns by maintaining transparency and involving the community in decision-making processes.

As the chapter nears its end, Thabo reflects on the journey of the soccer team. From a struggling local team, they have become a symbol of hope and a source of communal pride.

The impact of the team extends beyond sporting achievements; it has become a vehicle for social upliftment and unity.

"Uplifting the Township Team" is a testament to Thabo's vision and leadership. It illustrates how sports can be a powerful tool for social change, bringing together people from different backgrounds and instilling a sense of collective purpose and pride. The chapter closes with the township united in support of their team, a beacon of hope and a symbol of the potential inherent in every community.

As the township team garners more success and attention, Thabo's vision for a more cohesive and uplifted community begins to materialize. The soccer field becomes a hub of activity, not just for sports, but for community gatherings, cultural events, and educational workshops. Thabo's commitment to using soccer as a means for broader community development becomes increasingly evident.

The narrative shifts to focus on individual stories within the team - players who have overcome significant personal challenges and adversities. These stories, shared in community forums and local media, serve to inspire and motivate the youth in the township. The players are not just athletes; they become ambassadors of hope and resilience, embodying the potential that lies within each member of the community.

Thabo also realizes the importance of sustaining this momentum. He establishes a youth academy as part of the soccer club, aimed at nurturing young talent from an early age. The academy focuses on holistic development, providing education, life skills training, and soccer coaching. It becomes a beacon of opportunity, attracting youngsters who aspire to change their lives through sport.

In addition to nurturing young talent, Thabo emphasizes the importance of community engagement. He organizes events where the team players interact with local residents, sharing their experiences and encouraging community members to pursue their dreams, irrespective of their circumstances. These interactions foster a strong bond between the team and the community, with residents taking immense pride in the team's achievements.

The soccer team's influence begins to extend beyond the township. They start participating in national tournaments, showcasing their talent on larger stages. These opportunities bring new challenges and learning experiences for the team but also highlight the disparity in resources and support between teams from affluent areas and those from townships.

Thabo uses these experiences to advocate for more equitable support and resources in sports, especially for teams from underprivileged backgrounds. His efforts bring attention to the need for systemic changes in how sports are managed and funded at the national level.

As the chapter draws to a close, the township team clinches a significant victory in a national tournament, a moment of triumph that unites the entire community in celebration. This victory is more than just a sporting achievement; it symbolizes the breaking down of barriers and the realization of what can be achieved when a community comes together with a common purpose.

"Uplifting the Township Team" culminates in a celebratory scene, with the entire township coming out to welcome their heroes. The atmosphere is electric, filled with joy, pride, and a sense of collective accomplishment. Thabo stands amidst this celebration, not just as the architect of this success but as a member of a community that dared to dream big and turned those dreams into reality.

This chapter is a poignant reminder of the transformative power of sports and community. It celebrates the achievements of the township team while highlighting the ongoing struggles and challenges they face. Thabo's journey with the soccer team becomes a metaphor for hope, unity, and the relentless pursuit of excellence against all odds.

A COMMUNITY'S BEACON OF HOPE

A Community's Beacon of Hope, delves deeper into the transformative impact of Thabo Mokoena's soccer venture on the township. This chapter is a heartening portrayal of how the success of the soccer team becomes a source of inspiration and a catalyst for positive change within the community.

The chapter opens with the township still revelling in the afterglow of the team's recent victory. The streets buzz with excitement and a renewed sense of pride. Children are seen playing soccer in every available space, imitating their new heroes. Thabo's vision of using soccer as a tool for community upliftment is becoming a tangible reality.

Thabo, aware of the team's influence, takes proactive steps to leverage this momentum for greater community benefits. He starts by partnering with local schools, using the team's success to promote the importance of education and discipline. The players visit schools, share their stories, and participate in interactive sessions with students, emphasizing the values of hard work, teamwork, and perseverance.

The narrative then shifts to a significant development initiated by Thabo - the establishment of a community centre near the soccer field.

This centre becomes a hub for various activities: educational programs, vocational training, health awareness workshops, and cultural events. It's not just a physical space, but a symbol of hope and opportunity for the township residents.

Thabo also initiates community engagement projects through the soccer team. One such project is a mentorship program where team players mentor young people from the community. These mentorship relationships extend beyond soccer, focusing on personal development, career guidance, and life skills.

The impact of these initiatives is profound. The community starts to witness a decrease in youth involvement in negative activities. There's a noticeable increase in school attendance and performance, and more young people begin to express interest in pursuing higher education and vocational training.

However, Thabo's efforts are not without challenges. The chapter explores the resistance he faces from certain factions within the community who view his initiatives as an intrusion or as overshadowing other community needs. Thabo navigates these challenges with empathy and inclusivity, ensuring that the community's voice is heard and respected in all his initiatives.

A poignant moment in the chapter is when the soccer team organizes a charity match to raise funds for a local health clinic.

The event is a resounding success, drawing support from beyond the township and highlighting the power of sports in mobilizing resources for community causes.

As the chapter draws to a close, a sense of unity and optimism pervades the township. The soccer team's success has sparked a collective belief in the possibility of change and improvement. The residents, who once felt overlooked and marginalized, now have a renewed sense of agency and hope.

"A Community's Beacon of Hope" is a celebration of the positive ripple effects that one successful venture can have on an entire community. It illustrates how Thabo's soccer team, once just a group of local athletes, has evolved into a powerful force for social change. The chapter ends with Thabo looking over the bustling community centre, realizing that the team's legacy will extend far beyond the soccer field, embedding itself deeply into the fabric of the township's future.

In the wake of the community centre's success and the soccer team's growing influence, Thabo begins to see a transformation not only in individual lives but in the township's collective mindset. "A Community's Beacon of Hope" transitions into exploring how this transformation begins to reshape the township's future.

Thabo takes a moment to reflect on the journey so far. He sees young people who were once aimless now pursuing goals with determination, parents expressing pride in their children's achievements, and a general upliftment in the community's morale. The soccer team has become more than a sports entity; it's a symbol of unity and a source of communal pride.

The narrative then shifts to a new initiative spearheaded by Thabo – a local entrepreneurship program. Inspired by his own journey, Thabo encourages residents, especially the youth, to develop and pitch business ideas. The best ideas receive funding and mentorship from local business leaders, including Thabo himself. This program not only fosters a spirit of entrepreneurship but also creates a platform for economic development within the township.

An inspiring element in this chapter is the establishment of a soccer tournament for local teams, organized by Thabo and his team. This tournament is not just about sports; it's a celebration of community spirit, bringing together residents from all walks of life. Local businesses thrive as they cater to the crowds, and young talents from various townships get a chance to showcase their skills.

The team's influence extends to addressing social issues as well. Thabo uses the team's popularity to campaign for important causes like health awareness, education, and women's empowerment.

These campaigns are hugely successful, owing to the players' involvement and their connection with the community. However, Thabo remains aware of the need to balance growth with sustainability. He ensures that all initiatives are community-driven and are not solely dependent on the soccer team's success. He organizes workshops on community leadership and sustainability, aiming to build local capacity for managing and continuing these initiatives.

As the chapter nears its end, Thabo organizes a community celebration to mark the anniversary of the soccer team's first major victory. This event is more than a celebration of the team's success; it's a reflection of the community's journey. Stories of individual and collective achievements are shared, reinforcing the sense of community identity and strength.

"A Community's Beacon of Hope" concludes with a powerful scene of Thabo standing amidst the celebrations, watching the community he helped transform. He realizes that the true success of his journey lies not in trophies or accolades, but in the smiles, hopes, and aspirations of the township residents. This chapter is a testament to the idea that sports can be a powerful catalyst for community development and that one person's vision can ignite a collective journey towards hope and prosperity.

THE RISE TO PROMINENCE

The Rise to Prominence, chronicles a pivotal phase in Thabo Mokoena's journey as both the soccer team and his broader community initiatives begin to gain national recognition. This chapter explores the dynamics of success and its impact on Thabo, the team, and the township.

The chapter opens with the soccer team's unprecedented win in a national tournament, a victory that propels them into the national spotlight. This success is not just a triumph on the field; it symbolizes the potential of underrepresented communities and challenges long-standing stereotypes in the sports world.

As the team's fame grows, so does interest in Thabo's story. Media outlets across the country are eager to cover the remarkable tale of a tech entrepreneur turned community leader and soccer team patron. Thabo finds himself thrust into the public eye, a role he embraces with a mix of humility and strategic foresight.

Thabo uses this newfound prominence to amplify his message about the power of community-based initiatives and the potential lying dormant in townships like his. He becomes a sought-after speaker at national events, where he speaks not only about sports but also about entrepreneurship, social responsibility, and racial equity.

The narrative then shifts to how the soccer team's success begins to positively influence the township. The team's victories bring a sense of pride and collective identity to the residents, fostering a more cohesive community spirit. Young people, in particular, are inspired to pursue their passions, whether in sports, academics, or the arts.

Thabo's leadership style evolves as he navigates this rise to prominence. He becomes more than a community leader; he emerges as a national figure representing hope and change. Despite this, he remains deeply rooted in his community, ensuring that his initiatives continue to benefit the residents directly.

However, this rise to prominence also brings challenges. Thabo and the team face increased pressure to perform and maintain their success. The community's expectations rise, and Thabo feels the weight of being a role model for so many. Moreover, the spotlight brings scrutiny from critics and sceptics who question the sustainability of his initiatives and the team's success.

A significant part of the chapter is dedicated to Thabo's efforts to maintain the integrity of his mission amidst growing fame. He works tirelessly to ensure that the soccer team and community projects remain true to their original values. He focuses on building strong leadership within the community and the team, fostering a culture of self-reliance and sustainability.

The chapter concludes with a moment of reflection for Thabo. At a national award ceremony where he is honoured for his contributions, he looks out at the audience – a mix of prominent figures and community members – and realizes the vast impact of his work. From his humble beginnings to national acclaim, Thabo's journey symbolizes the limitless potential of dedication, vision, and community spirit.

"The Rise to Prominence" is a celebration of success and its ripple effects across various spheres. It portrays Thabo's journey as a beacon of hope and a testament to the power of unwavering commitment to one's roots and values in the face of fame and recognition.

As the event concludes and the crowds begin to disperse, Thabo takes a moment to soak in the atmosphere. He feels a deep connection to the community, a sense of accomplishment mingled with an overwhelming sense of responsibility for what comes next. The chapter, "The Rise to Prominence," thus transitions into a phase of introspection and forward planning.

In the days following the event, Thabo reflects on the broader impact of his initiatives. He realizes that while the soccer team and the community projects have achieved remarkable success, there is still much work to be done. He begins to envision a more integrated approach to community development, one that combines sports, education, entrepreneurship, and health into a cohesive strategy.

The narrative then shifts to Thabo's efforts in bringing this integrated approach to life. He collaborates with local leaders, businesses, and international organizations to develop comprehensive programs that address various aspects of community life. These programs focus not only on immediate needs but also on long-term sustainability and self-sufficiency.

One of the key initiatives Thabo introduces is a community-led governance model for the various programs. This model involves residents in decision-making processes, ensuring that the initiatives align with the community's needs and aspirations. Thabo believes that for lasting change to occur, the community must be at the forefront, driving the development.

The soccer team, meanwhile, continues to thrive, becoming a symbol of excellence and a source of inspiration far beyond the township. The players, many of whom have become local celebrities, use their influence to advocate for community issues and participate actively in Thabo's initiatives. Their success story reinforces the message that talent and potential exist in the most unexpected places.

However, Thabo's journey is not without its hurdles. With increased visibility and influence come heightened expectations and scrutiny. He faces challenges in balancing the various aspects of his work, ensuring that neither his business interests nor his community commitments are neglected.

A poignant part of the chapter is when Thabo revisits his childhood home, walking through the streets of the township. The visit serves as a powerful reminder of his roots and the initial motivations for his journey. Conversations with old friends and neighbours rekindle his passion and reinforce his commitment to the community's welfare.

As the chapter draws to a close, Thabo is seen planning a series of town hall meetings to discuss future projects and gather feedback from the community. He remains deeply engaged with the residents, ensuring that his work continues to reflect the community's needs and aspirations.

"The Rise to Prominence" ends with Thabo looking ahead, ready to tackle the next phase of his journey. He recognizes that his role has evolved from being just a leader to a facilitator of community empowerment. The chapter closes with a sense of anticipation and hope, as Thabo prepares to embark on new initiatives that will further uplift the community and solidify its place as a beacon of hope and progress.

JEALOUSY AMONG THE ELITES

Jealousy Among the Elites, explores a new set of challenges that arise as Thabo Mokoena's initiatives gain more prominence. The chapter delves into the complexities of navigating success in a landscape where not all are pleased with the shifting status quo.

As Thabo's community projects and the soccer team continue to flourish, garnering national acclaim, they inadvertently attract the attention of some influential figures in the business and sports world. While many admire and support Thabo's work, a faction of the elite views his rising influence with unease and jealousy.

The chapter opens with Thabo becoming aware of subtle, yet growing, resistance from certain high-profile individuals. These individuals, entrenched in the traditional power structures, feel threatened by Thabo's unconventional approach and his growing popularity. They are wary of the attention he is drawing to the township and the empowerment it brings to its residents.

Thabo encounters instances of this jealousy manifesting in various forms. There are attempts to undermine his projects through bureaucratic red tape, influential figures in the sports industry casting doubt on the legitimacy of the soccer team's success, and business leaders questioning the viability and motives of his community development initiatives.

One significant incident that exemplifies this jealousy is when a well-established sports organization begins to question the eligibility of some of Thabo's soccer team players, alleging rule violations. Thabo sees this as a thinly veiled attempt to discredit the team's achievements and to dampen the spirits of the township.

Despite these challenges, Thabo remains undeterred. He understands that these reactions are part of a broader resistance to change. He navigates these obstacles with a combination of diplomacy and firmness, always prioritizing the welfare of his community and the integrity of his projects.

The narrative also explores how Thabo's team and the community react to these external pressures. There is a sense of indignation and a rallying of support for Thabo. The community's unity becomes stronger, and the soccer team players become more determined to prove their critics wrong.

Amidst this turmoil, Thabo continues to advocate for fair treatment and equal opportunities. He uses his platform to speak out against the systemic biases and challenges that his initiatives face, drawing attention to the broader issues of inequality and social justice.

As the chapter progresses, Thabo's efforts to counter these challenges bear fruit. The allegations against the soccer team are proven unfounded, and the team's right to their victories is upheld.

This victory is not just a win for the team but a symbolic triumph for the community against the odds stacked against them.

The chapter concludes with Thabo reflecting on the nature of success and the inevitability of opposition. He realizes that the path he has chosen is fraught with challenges, but it is also one that brings meaningful change. "Jealousy Among the Elites" ends with Thabo more resolute than ever to continue his work, bolstered by the unwavering support of his community and the undeniable impact of his initiatives.

In the wake of these challenges, Thabo becomes more aware of the delicate balance between progress and resistance. "Jealousy Among the Elites" thus transitions into exploring how Thabo navigates these newfound complexities while maintaining his focus on community upliftment.

Despite clearing the team of allegations, the incident leaves Thabo contemplative about the broader implications of his work. He recognizes that his initiatives, while beneficial to his community, are disrupting established power dynamics, leading to resistance from those with vested interests in maintaining the status quo.

The narrative shifts to highlight Thabo's strategic approach in dealing with this resistance. He realizes that direct confrontation might not always be the most effective strategy. Instead, he opts for engagement and dialogue, seeking to build bridges where possible. Thabo starts reaching out to some of the influential figures who have shown resistance, aiming to find common ground and mutual understanding.

A crucial part of the chapter is when Thabo organizes a roundtable discussion with various stakeholders, including his critics. The event is a platform for open dialogue about the challenges and opportunities presented by his initiatives. Thabo's aim is to create a shared vision for the community's development, one that includes diverse perspectives and interests.

This event proves to be a turning point. While not all differences are resolved, there is a newfound respect for Thabo's work and an acknowledgment of its impact. Some of the elites begin to see the potential benefits of supporting his initiatives, both for the community and their interests.

Thabo also becomes more astute in navigating the political landscape. He partners with like-minded organizations and individuals, building a broader coalition of support. These partnerships help to bolster his initiatives and provide a buffer against future challenges.

The chapter also delves into the personal impact of these challenges on Thabo. The resistance he faces takes a toll, leading to moments of doubt and frustration. However, these feelings are counterbalanced by the support and trust of his community. Their faith in him serves as a constant reminder of why he started this journey.

As "Jealousy Among the Elites" draws to a close, Thabo finds himself at a crossroads. The success of his initiatives has brought him into a realm of higher stakes and greater responsibilities. He is more determined than ever to continue his work, but with a deeper understanding of the complexities involved in challenging entrenched systems.

The chapter ends with Thabo looking out over the township, reflecting on the journey so far. He sees a community that has grown stronger and more united, a testament to the power of collective effort. This sight reaffirms his commitment to continue pushing for change, no matter the resistance he faces. Thabo's journey thus evolves from a story of individual success to one of communal resilience and the power of unity in the face of adversity.

CONSPIRACY SHADOWS

Conspiracy Shadows, the narrative takes a darker turn as Thabo Mokoena begins to uncover a web of conspiracy aimed at undermining his initiatives and discrediting his achievements. This chapter delves into the intrigue and challenges that come with confronting hidden adversaries.

The chapter opens with a series of unexplained setbacks and challenges facing both Thabo's community projects and the soccer team. Equipment for the team goes missing, funding for a community program is suddenly withdrawn, and rumours start to circulate questioning the integrity of Thabo's initiatives. These incidents seem isolated at first, but Thabo starts to suspect a coordinated effort to sabotage his work.

Thabo's suspicions are confirmed when an anonymous source contact him, hinting at a conspiracy by a group of influential figures who feel threatened by his success and the empowerment of the township. These figures are described as having significant sway in business and political circles and are purportedly using their influence to stymie Thabo's efforts.

The narrative then shifts to Thabo's response to these revelations. Initially shocked and disheartened, he quickly regroups, determined to uncover the truth and protect his community's interests.

He starts an informal investigation, enlisting the help of trusted friends and associates to gather information and piece together the puzzle. As Thabo delves deeper into the investigation, the extent of the conspiracy becomes more apparent. It's not just about jealousy or resistance to change; it's a concerted effort to maintain control and power dynamics that Thabo's initiatives are challenging. The conspirators are using underhanded tactics, leveraging their networks to create obstacles and spread misinformation.

A significant part of the chapter is dedicated to a tense encounter between Thabo and one of the alleged conspirators, a high-profile business leader. The meeting is fraught with veiled threats and accusations, but Thabo stands his ground, making it clear that he will not be intimidated or deterred from his mission.

Despite the gravity of the situation, Thabo remains committed to handling the matter with discretion and integrity. He understands that publicizing the conspiracy without concrete proof could cause unnecessary panic and harm the community's morale. His approach is to gather irrefutable evidence before taking any public action.

As Thabo continues his investigation, the impact of the conspiracy on his initiatives becomes more pronounced. The community starts to feel the strain, with some residents growing doubtful and fearful. Thabo realizes that he needs to act quickly to counter the negative impact and to reaffirm the community's trust in his leadership.

The chapter concludes with Thabo organizing a community meeting to address the growing concerns. He speaks candidly about the challenges they are facing, without revealing the full extent of the conspiracy. His message is one of unity and resilience, urging the community to stand together in the face of adversity.

"Conspiracy Shadows" ends with Thabo more determined than ever to protect his community and to bring the conspirators to light. The chapter sets the stage for a deeper exploration of the struggle against hidden forces of opposition, highlighting Thabo's resolve and the community's unwavering support in the face of covert challenges.
The tension in the township is palpable as "Conspiracy Shadows" progresses. Thabo's efforts to unravel the conspiracy against him and his initiatives take on a more urgent tone. He finds himself in a delicate situation, needing to protect his community and their achievements while confronting the powerful forces aligned against them.

Thabo's strategy involves a careful balancing act. He continues to gather evidence discreetly, collaborating with a small, trusted group. This team works meticulously, tracing the origins of the rumours and the sudden setbacks they've faced. They start to connect the dots, linking the incidents to a network of influential individuals who are covertly orchestrating the opposition.

Meanwhile, Thabo maintains a strong front in public. He continues to champion his initiatives, rallying the community around their shared goals and successes. He uses community meetings, local media, and public events to reinforce the positive impact of their work, countering the negative narrative being spun by the conspirators.

An important subplot in the chapter is the impact of the conspiracy on the soccer team. The players, aware of the challenges, face a crisis of morale. Thabo steps in, offering support and guidance. He shares with them the importance of resilience and unity in the face of adversity. His leadership helps to galvanize the team, turning their anxiety into a renewed determination to succeed.

As Thabo's investigation deepens, he uncovers the full extent of the conspiracy. It's not just local; it has connections extending to regional and even national levels. This revelation is alarming, but it also gives Thabo the clarity he needs to formulate his response.

The chapter reaches a climax when Thabo and his team manage to obtain concrete evidence of the conspiracy. This evidence includes communication records and financial transactions that clearly implicate the conspirators. Armed with this information, Thabo must make a critical decision on how to proceed.

After much deliberation, Thabo decides to confront the situation head-on. He arranges a meeting with the key figures involved in the conspiracy, presenting them with the evidence he has gathered. The meeting is tense, with Thabo standing firm in the face of intimidation and threats. He makes it clear that he is prepared to take legal action if necessary but also offers a chance for reconciliation and collaboration, echoing his belief in dialogue and community cohesion.

The chapter ends on a note of cautious optimism. The conspirators, realizing that Thabo is not easily intimidated and that he has the community's support, agree to cease their opposition. Thabo, for his part, agrees to engage in a dialogue with them to find common ground for the benefit of the broader community.

"Conspiracy Shadows" concludes with Thabo reflecting on the challenges he has faced and the resilience he and his community have shown. He understands that the path to change is fraught with obstacles, but the solidarity and strength of his community give him the courage to continue. The chapter sets the stage for further developments in Thabo's journey, highlighting his strategic acumen, commitment to his values, and the unwavering support of his community.

THE BANK SCANDAL UNFOLDS

The Bank Scandal Unfolds, Thabo Mokoena's journey takes an unexpected turn as he finds himself entangled in a financial scandal that threatens to undermine all his achievements. This chapter explores themes of betrayal, resilience, and the quest for justice.

The chapter begins with a sudden crisis. Thabo is informed by his bank that there are irregularities in the financial accounts of his community projects and the soccer team. Initially, Thabo believes this to be a misunderstanding or a clerical error. However, as he delves deeper, he realizes the gravity of the situation. Large sums of money have been embezzled, and all evidence points towards Thabo and his management team.

Thabo is shocked and confused. He struggles to comprehend how this could have happened under his watch. The scandal quickly becomes public, and the media pounce on the story, casting a shadow of doubt over Thabo's integrity and his initiatives. The community is stunned, and the trust that Thabo had worked so hard to build starts to crumble.

As Thabo grapples with the unfolding scandal, he discovers that the conspiracy he had previously uncovered may be connected to this new crisis. He suspects that the financial irregularities have been orchestrated to discredit him and destabilize the community projects.

The narrative shifts to Thabo's efforts to clear his name and uncover the truth. He enlists the help of a reputable accounting firm to conduct an independent audit of the finances. Simultaneously, he works with a legal team to investigate the embezzlement and to prepare for any potential legal battles.

The investigation reveals a complex web of deceit involving several high-ranking individuals in the banking institution. These individuals had exploited their positions to manipulate the accounts and frame Thabo. The motive, it becomes clear, is rooted in the same jealousy and resistance to change that had fuelled the earlier conspiracy.

As the scandal unfolds, Thabo faces immense public scrutiny and personal stress. He struggles to maintain his focus on his community projects, which suffer from the negative publicity and financial strain caused by the scandal. The soccer team, too, feels the impact, with sponsors withdrawing their support and morale plummeting.

A pivotal moment in the chapter occurs when Thabo holds a press conference to address the allegations. He speaks candidly about the situation, maintaining his innocence and outlining the steps he has taken to resolve the issue. His transparency and humility in facing the crisis resonate with many, and he begins to regain some of the lost public trust.

The chapter concludes with the independent audit exonerating Thabo and his team. The real perpetrators are identified and legal action is initiated against them. While this is a significant victory for Thabo, the damage done to his reputation and to his community initiatives is substantial.

"The Bank Scandal Unfolds" is a chapter that tests Thabo's resilience and integrity. It highlights the challenges of navigating success in a landscape marked by envy and corruption. The chapter ends with Thabo reflecting on the lessons learned and his renewed commitment to rebuilding trust and continuing his work for the community.

As Thabo begins the process of rebuilding in the aftermath of the scandal, "The Bank Scandal Unfolds" transitions into a phase of recovery and introspection.

The exoneration brings a sense of relief to Thabo, but the ordeal leaves lingering effects. The community's trust in his initiatives has been shaken, and the morale of the soccer team has taken a hit. Thabo realizes that he needs to take proactive steps not just to repair the damage but to strengthen the foundations of his projects to prevent future vulnerabilities.

One of Thabo's first actions is to organize a series of community meetings. He understands the importance of open communication and transparency in restoring trust. During these meetings, Thabo listens to the concerns and suggestions of the community members. He acknowledges the setbacks and reassures them of his commitment to the community's welfare and the success of their collective initiatives.

Thabo also takes steps to strengthen the financial management and oversight of his projects. He implements new checks and balances, introduces more stringent auditing processes, and involves community representatives in financial planning and monitoring. These measures are designed to ensure transparency and to rebuild confidence among stakeholders and sponsors.

In parallel, Thabo focuses on revitalizing the soccer team. He organizes team-building activities and motivational sessions to boost morale. He also works on securing new sponsorships, leveraging the team's past successes and the recent vindication to rebuild their reputation and attract support.

A significant part of the chapter is dedicated to Thabo's personal reflections and growth. The scandal has been a humbling experience for him, highlighting vulnerabilities he hadn't previously considered. It reinforces his resolve to be more vigilant and involved in all aspects of his initiatives, especially in areas where he had delegated responsibilities.

Thabo's resilience in the face of this crisis starts to inspire renewed optimism in the community. Slowly, the shadow cast by the scandal begins to lift. The community projects start to regain momentum, and the soccer team finds its stride again, performing well in local and regional tournaments.

The chapter also explores the broader impact of Thabo's vindication. It serves as a powerful example of integrity and perseverance against false accusations. Thabo's story becomes a source of inspiration for other community leaders facing similar challenges. It highlights the importance of resilience, transparency, and community solidarity in overcoming adversity.

As "The Bank Scandal Unfolds" concludes, Thabo stands as a more seasoned, cautious, yet undeterred leader. He reaffirms his dedication to his community and his initiatives, now with a deeper understanding of the challenges and complexities of leading change. The chapter closes with a sense of cautious hope and renewed purpose, setting the stage for the next phase of Thabo's journey in uplifting his community.

CAUGHT IN A WEB OF DECEIT

Caught in a Web of Deceit, delves into the aftermath of the bank scandal, highlighting Thabo Mokoena's struggles to navigate the lingering mistrust and the intricate web of deceit that still surrounds his initiatives.

The chapter opens with Thabo reflecting on the scandal's impact. Despite being exonerated, the residue of suspicion and doubt continues to affect him personally and professionally. He finds himself questioning the loyalty and motives of those around him, a sentiment that is mirrored in the community's cautious approach to his projects.

Thabo's leadership is further challenged when he uncovers additional layers of deceit within his own network. He discovers that a close associate, someone he had trusted implicitly, was indirectly involved in the scandal. This betrayal hits Thabo hard, shaking the very foundations of his trust and forcing him to re-evaluate his relationships and management approach.

The narrative then shifts to Thabo's efforts to untangle this web of deceit. He realizes that to move forward, he must confront and resolve these internal issues. Thabo initiates a thorough review of his team and projects, determined to root out any remaining elements of corruption or betrayal.

As Thabo delves deeper, he uncovers a complex network of alliances and backdoor dealings that had subtly influenced his projects. These revelations are difficult to digest, but they provide Thabo with a clearer understanding of the challenges he faces in trying to effect change within a corrupt system.

The chapter also explores the impact of these revelations on the community. The news of the internal betrayal causes disillusionment and anger. Thabo faces the challenging task of restoring faith not only in his leadership but also in the potential for genuine progress within the community.

Amidst this turmoil, Thabo works tirelessly to reinforce the integrity of his initiatives. He introduces more robust governance structures, fosters a culture of transparency, and encourages open dialogue within his team and the community. He also takes steps to personally reconnect with the community, participating in local events and informal gatherings to listen to and address their concerns.

A pivotal moment in the chapter is when Thabo organizes a large town hall meeting. He addresses the community openly about the challenges they have faced, the steps taken to address them, and his vision for moving forward. Thabo's honesty and vulnerability in this meeting resonate with the community, helping to mend some of the trust that was broken.

As the chapter draws to a close, Thabo begins to see small but significant signs of recovery. The community's engagement in his projects gradually increases, and the soccer team starts to regain its former glory, symbolizing a renewed sense of hope and resilience.

"Caught in a Web of Deceit" is a chapter about confronting and overcoming internal challenges and betrayals. It highlights the importance of resilience, transparency, and ethical leadership in navigating complex social and professional landscapes. The chapter ends with Thabo, more determined and vigilant than ever, continuing his journey to uplift his community against all odds.

The resolution of the internal turmoil marks the beginning of a new chapter for Thabo and his initiatives. In "Caught in a Web of Deceit," Thabo's journey evolves from confronting external threats to addressing internal vulnerabilities, reinforcing the resilience and integrity of his mission.

As Thabo works to rebuild trust and strengthen his initiatives, he becomes more introspective about his leadership style. He recognizes that while his vision and dedication have been driving forces, they also made him overlook potential weaknesses within his own team. This realization leads Thabo to foster a more inclusive and participatory leadership approach, where feedback and diverse perspectives are actively encouraged.

The chapter then explores Thabo's efforts to revitalize the community projects and the soccer team. He initiates new community engagement programs, focusing on inclusivity and transparency. These programs are designed to not only advance the projects but also to rebuild the sense of community ownership and pride that had been dampened by the scandal.

A significant development in this chapter is Thabo's decision to establish an advisory board for his initiatives. This board includes respected community members, business leaders, and representatives from various local organizations. Its purpose is to provide oversight, guidance, and a diversity of perspectives, ensuring that the initiatives remain aligned with community needs and values.

Thabo also dedicates time to mentoring young leaders within the community, recognizing the importance of nurturing a new generation of changemakers. He shares his experiences, both successes and failures, to inspire and educate these emerging leaders.

The narrative highlights a key event where the soccer team participates in a high-profile tournament. The team's performance, marked by skill and sportsmanship, reflects the renewed spirit and resilience they have developed. Their success at the tournament becomes a symbol of the community's comeback from the recent challenges.

As the chapter nears its conclusion, Thabo reflects on the lessons learned from the recent turmoil. He understands that true leadership involves not only guiding others to success but also learning from them and adapting to challenges. The community, once shaken by the scandal, now stands stronger and more united, their faith in Thabo's leadership restored.

"Caught in a Web of Deceit" concludes with Thabo looking ahead, ready to embark on the next phase of his journey with a renewed sense of purpose and wisdom. The chapter sets the stage for further developments in Thabo's initiatives, highlighting his commitment to ethical leadership, community empowerment, and the relentless pursuit of positive change.

PUBLIC FALL FROM GRACE

Public Fall from Grace, narrates a pivotal and challenging period in Thabo Mokoena's life, where despite his efforts to rebuild, he faces a significant setback that tarnishes his public image and tests his resolve.

The chapter begins with an unexpected turn of events. A misunderstanding involving one of Thabo's new community projects escalates quickly, fuelled by rumours and misinformation. The media, still vigilant from the previous bank scandal, seizes upon this issue, casting it in a sensational light. The situation is blown out of proportion, leading to a public outcry against Thabo and his initiatives.

Thabo finds himself at the centre of a controversy that he struggles to comprehend and control. The negative media coverage spreads rapidly, painting him as a figure who has mis-used his position and influence for personal gain. These narrative gains traction, overshadowing Thabo's past achievements and the positive impact of his work.

As Thabo grapples with this public relations crisis, he experiences a profound sense of isolation and betrayal. Some members of the community, swayed by the media portrayal, begin to distance themselves from him. Sponsors withdraw their support, and key partners reconsider their associations with his projects.

The narrative delves into Thabo's emotional turmoil during this period. He feels a deep sense of injustice, knowing that the accusations are based on misunderstandings and misrepresentations. However, he also introspects on whether his actions, however well-intentioned, might have contributed to the situation.

Thabo's leadership and resilience are put to the test as he navigates this fall from grace. He reaches out to community leaders, former allies, and the media to clarify the situation, but finds that his efforts are met with scepticism and resistance. The trust and goodwill he had worked so hard to build seem to evaporate overnight.

In a pivotal scene, Thabo holds a press conference to address the accusations directly. He speaks candidly about the situation, acknowledging any missteps and reaffirming his commitment to the community's welfare. Despite his sincere efforts, the damage to his reputation is significant, and the path to redemption appears arduous.

The chapter also explores the impact of this crisis on Thabo's personal life. He faces stress and anxiety, which strain his relationships with family and close friends. The unwavering support of his family becomes a crucial anchor in these turbulent times, reminding him of the values and motivations that inspired his journey.

As "Public Fall from Grace" concludes, Thabo is left to contemplate the future of his initiatives and his role within the community. The chapter ends on a note of uncertainty but also determination.

Thabo realizes that his journey is not just about achieving success but also about enduring and learning from setbacks. He resolves to continue his work, albeit with a more cautious and reflective approach, understanding that the path to rebuilding trust and regaining his stature will be a challenging one.

In the wake of his public fall from grace, Thabo Mokoena finds himself at a critical crossroads. The transitions into a period of introspection and resilience as Thabo confronts the biggest challenge of his journey thus far.

Thabo's initial response to the crisis is to retreat from the public eye, using this time to reflect and reassess his approach. He recognizes that while his intentions have always been for the betterment of his community, the execution of his projects might have lacked the necessary transparency and oversight to prevent misunderstandings.

During this period, Thabo engages in deep conversations with his family, close friends, and trusted advisors. These discussions are candid, sometimes uncomfortable, but they provide Thabo with much-needed perspective and guidance.

He begins to understand the importance of not only having a vision but also effectively communicating it and involving the community in every step of the process.

A significant part of the chapter focuses on Thabo's efforts to reconnect with his community. He starts attending local gatherings and events, not as a leader but as a member of the community, listening more and speaking less. These interactions are humbling for Thabo, but they also rekindle his connection with the community and remind him of why he started his journey.

Thabo also takes concrete steps to address the issues that led to his fall from grace. He works with a team of experts to establish stronger governance structures for his projects. These structures include clear protocols for financial management, regular audits, and community oversight committees to ensure transparency and accountability.

The narrative then shifts to a small yet significant victory for Thabo. A community project that had been stalled due to the controversy gets revived, thanks to the efforts of a group of community members who still believe in Thabo's vision. This event is a turning point, signalling a slow but steady resurgence of support for Thabo's initiatives.

As Thabo starts to rebuild his reputation, he faces a mix of scepticism and encouragement. Some members of the community remain wary, their trust eroded by the media portrayal of Thabo.

Others, however, begin to see the changes Thabo is implementing and slowly start to rally around him again.

The chapter concludes with Thabo organizing a community forum, where he openly addresses the past issues, discusses the changes he has implemented, and invites feedback and suggestions from the community. The forum is well-attended, and while there are moments of tension, it ends on a hopeful note, with many expressing their willingness to give Thabo and his initiatives a second chance.

"Public Fall from Grace" is a chapter about the complexities of leadership, the importance of community trust, and the resilience needed to overcome setbacks. It ends with Thabo emerging as a more humble, reflective, and determined leader, ready to continue his journey with a renewed sense of purpose and understanding.

ASSET CONFISCATION: THE TAKEDOWN

Asset Confiscation: The Takedown, marks a dramatic escalation in Thabo Mokoena's challenges, as he faces the severe consequences of the ongoing controversies and scandals.

The chapter begins with a startling development: due to the unresolved financial irregularities and the ensuing scandal, authorities initiate a process of asset confiscation against Thabo. This move is a severe blow to Thabo, both personally and professionally. The assets in question include not only his personal properties but also the facilities and equipment used for his community projects and the soccer team.

Thabo is stunned by this development. The confiscation represents not just a financial loss but also a symbolic defeat, stripping away the very tools and resources he had used to uplift his community. The impact on the community is immediate and devastating. Projects come to a halt, the soccer team loses its training ground, and the sense of hope and progress that Thabo had worked so hard to instil begins to fade.

The narrative delves into the legal and emotional turmoil that Thabo experiences. He finds himself entangled in a complex legal battle to prove his innocence and reclaim the confiscated assets. The process is exhausting and demoralizing, as Thabo has to navigate a maze of bureaucratic procedures and legal technicalities.

Amidst this struggle, Thabo's resilience is put to the test. He faces public humiliation and the disappointment of those who had believed in him. The media scrutiny is relentless, and Thabo finds himself isolated, with former allies and supporters distancing themselves from him.

Despite these challenges, Thabo refuses to give up. He clings to the belief that justice will prevail and that he will be able to restore his name and continue his work for the community. He spends countless hours with his legal team, working on his defence and seeking ways to reverse the asset confiscation.

A significant part of the chapter focuses on the emotional toll this situation takes on Thabo. He grapples with feelings of anger, frustration, and despair. However, in these dark moments, Thabo also finds moments of clarity and determination. He begins to see this challenge not just as a personal battle but as a symbol of the struggles faced by many in his community against systemic injustices.

As the legal battle drags on, Thabo receives unexpected support from a segment of the community. A grassroots movement begins to form, rallying behind Thabo and protesting against what they see as an unjust takedown of a community leader. This support provides Thabo with a glimmer of hope and a reminder of the impact he has had on the lives of many.

The chapter concludes without a resolution to the legal battle, leaving Thabo's fate and the future of his initiatives uncertain. However, it ends with a powerful scene of Thabo standing amidst a group of community supporters, realizing that his journey has ignited a larger conversation about justice, resilience, and the power of community solidarity.

"Asset Confiscation: The Takedown" is a sobering chapter that explores the depths of Thabo's challenges and the strength of his character. It sets the stage for a continued fight for justice and the reclamation of his life's work.

In "Asset Confiscation: The Takedown," Thabo Mokoena's journey becomes emblematic of a larger struggle, as he grapples with the repercussions of the asset confiscation and the ongoing legal battles.

As Thabo continues to fight for the return of his assets, the narrative explores the solidarity and resilience within the community. The grassroots movement supporting Thabo gains momentum, organizing rallies and fundraisers. This groundswell of support is not just about aiding Thabo; it evolves into a broader campaign against systemic injustice and for community empowerment.

Meanwhile, Thabo's legal team works tirelessly, uncovering flaws in the asset confiscation process and challenging the allegations against Thabo.

The legal proceedings are complex and fraught with setbacks, but they slowly begin to uncover the truth behind the financial irregularities that led to Thabo's downfall.

The chapter also delves into Thabo's personal journey during this tumultuous period. He faces moments of doubt and despair, feeling the weight of the situation on his shoulders. However, the community's support and his own inner resilience keep him going. Thabo spends time reflecting on his path, learning from his mistakes, and drawing strength from the adversity he faces.

A turning point in the chapter occurs when new evidence comes to light, suggesting that the asset confiscation was part of a larger scheme to discredit Thabo and dismantle his community projects. This revelation galvanizes Thabo and his supporters, adding credence to their claims of injustice and rallying more support to their cause.

The narrative then shifts to a crucial court hearing. Thabo's legal team presents the new evidence, challenging the legality of the asset confiscation. The courtroom is packed with Thabo's supporters, reflecting the community's vested interest in the outcome.

As the chapter nears its conclusion, the judge announces a decision in Thabo's favour. The court finds that the asset confiscation was indeed unjust and orders the return of Thabo's assets.

This victory is a significant moment for Thabo and the community; it represents a triumph over adversity and a vindication of Thabo's integrity.

The chapter ends with a community celebration. Thabo, surrounded by supporters, feels a renewed sense of purpose and hope. He realizes that the journey ahead will be challenging, but he is now armed with a stronger sense of community support and a reaffirmed commitment to his vision.

"Asset Confiscation: The Takedown" is a chapter of struggle and triumph. It highlights the importance of community, the power of resilience, and the impact of collective action in the face of injustice. The chapter sets the stage for Thabo's continued journey, now bolstered by a deeper connection with his community and a clearer vision for the future.

THE DARKNESS OF DESPAIR

The Darkness of Despair, delves into a period of profound challenge and introspection for Thabo Mokoena, following the tumultuous events of the asset confiscation and his subsequent legal victory. Despite the triumph in court, Thabo faces a personal and emotional struggle that tests his resilience and conviction.

The chapter begins with Thabo experiencing a sense of emptiness and exhaustion. The prolonged legal battle and the relentless public scrutiny have taken a toll on him. While he has regained his assets and a degree of vindication, the ordeal has left him questioning the very essence of his mission and his future role in the community.

Thabo finds himself in a state of isolation, withdrawing from public engagements and community activities. He grapples with feelings of disillusionment and a loss of purpose. The once vibrant and passionate leader now struggles with a pervasive sense of hopelessness, questioning whether his efforts have truly made a difference.

The narrative explores Thabo's internal battle as he confronts these feelings of despair. He reflects on the journey he has undertaken, the successes he has achieved, and the setbacks he has endured. The loneliness of leadership weighs heavily on him, and he feels a deep sense of responsibility for the challenges his community has faced.

In this period of introspection, Thabo also contends with strained personal relationships. His family and close friends are concerned about his well-being, but Thabo feels distant, unable to articulate his inner turmoil. The support network that he once relied on seems distant as he navigates this personal crisis.

The chapter then shifts to a poignant moment where Thabo visits the soccer field, once a source of joy and pride, now a symbol of his unfulfilled aspirations. As he watches a group of children playing on the field, Thabo is reminded of the reasons he embarked on his journey – to empower his community and provide opportunities for the next generation.

This moment at the soccer field becomes a turning point for Thabo. He begins to realize that while he cannot control every aspect of his journey, he can choose how to respond to the challenges. This realization sparks a slow but steady resurgence of his determination and passion.

Thabo starts to re-engage with his community, albeit more cautiously. He participates in small local events and spends time listening to the stories and experiences of community members. These interactions gradually help to restore his sense of connection and purpose.

As "The Darkness of Despair" concludes, Thabo is on the path to recovery, both emotionally and spiritually. He acknowledges that the journey ahead will be fraught with challenges, but he is now more equipped to face them.

The chapter ends with a sense of cautious hope, as Thabo reaffirms his commitment to his community and his vision, recognizing that true resilience lies in the ability to rise from the depths of despair and continue the fight for a better future.

As Thabo Mokoena navigates through "The Darkness of Despair," he finds himself in a profound state of introspection and solitude. This chapter continues to explore his journey as he grapples with the aftermath of his legal victory and the persistent challenges facing his initiatives.

The isolation and emotional toll of his struggles begin to manifest more deeply. Thabo, once a pillar of strength and optimism in his community, now wrestles with feelings of doubt and a loss of direction. The relentless pressures and public scrutiny have left him questioning his impact and the future of his work.

In these moments of despair, Thabo retreats from the public eye, seeking solace in the quieter parts of his life. He spends time alone, reflecting on his journey, the decisions he has made, and the sacrifices he has endured. The burden of leadership weighs heavily on him, and he begins to wonder if his efforts have been in vain.

The narrative delves into Thabo's struggle to reconcile his ideals with the harsh realities he has faced. The sense of betrayal and the erosion of trust have impacted him deeply, challenging his core beliefs about community, leadership, and change.

As Thabo grapples with these challenges, he starts to disconnect from the projects and people he once passionately led. His absence is felt in the community, where his guidance and vision were once driving forces. The soccer team, the community projects, and the various initiatives he spearheaded feel the void left by his retreat.

Amidst this personal crisis, a glimmer of hope emerges. Thabo receives unexpected support from unlikely sources. Small groups within the community, individuals whose lives have been positively impacted by his work, begin to reach out. They share stories of how Thabo's initiatives have changed their lives, offering words of encouragement and gratitude.

These interactions, though small, begin to pierce the veil of despair that has shrouded Thabo. He is reminded that his work, despite the challenges and setbacks, has made a real difference in people's lives. This realization becomes a beacon of light in his darkness, slowly rekindling his sense of purpose.

"The Darkness of Despair" concludes with Thabo taking tentative steps to re-engage with his community. He starts by attending a local soccer match, where he is greeted with warmth and respect. The experience is bittersweet, filled with memories of better times, but it also serves as a reminder of the joy and unity that the sport brings to the community.

The chapter ends with Thabo standing on the side-lines of the soccer field after the match, watching the sunset. In this moment of quiet reflection, he realizes that his journey is far from over. The path ahead may be uncertain and fraught with challenges, but his commitment to his community and his vision remains undiminished. Thabo's story of despair thus transforms into a narrative of resilience and renewed hope.

A PRISONER OF INJUSTICE

A Prisoner of Injustice, delves into a new, harrowing phase of Thabo Mokoena's journey. Despite his efforts to rebuild and reconnect, Thabo finds himself ensnared in a legal quagmire that threatens his freedom and further tests his resolve.

The chapter opens with a shocking development: Thabo is arrested on allegations of corruption and embezzlement related to his community projects. These charges, stemming from the tangled aftermath of the previous scandals and the asset confiscation, catch Thabo and the community off guard. The arrest is a public spectacle, further damaging Thabo's reputation and casting a shadow over his initiatives.

Thabo's incarceration is a jarring experience. He finds himself in a world far removed from the community he has dedicated his life to serving. The stark reality of the prison environment, coupled with the sense of injustice, weighs heavily on him. He grapples with feelings of anger, betrayal, and helplessness.

Inside prison, Thabo is forced to confront the harsh realities of the justice system and the disparities it often presents. He meets other inmates who share stories of similar experiences of injustice and wrongful imprisonment. These interactions open Thabo's eyes to broader systemic issues and reinforce his resolve to fight not only for his freedom but also for justice and fairness.

The narrative then shifts to the community's reaction to Thabo's arrest. There is a sense of shock and disbelief, followed by a mobilization of support. Rallies and protests are organized, calling for Thabo's release and highlighting the perceived injustices in his case. The soccer team, which Thabo nurtured, becomes a vocal advocate for his cause, using their games and public platform to draw attention to his plight.

Meanwhile, Thabo's legal team works tirelessly to contest the charges and secure his release. They face numerous obstacles, from bureaucratic delays to a lack of evidence to conclusively prove Thabo's innocence. The legal battle is fraught with setbacks, but the team remains determined, driven by a belief in Thabo's integrity and the injustice of his situation.

As Thabo endures his time in prison, he undergoes a profound transformation. The experience deepens his understanding of social injustices and the plight of those who are voiceless in the face of systemic oppression. He begins to envision new ways to address these issues, contemplating how his initiatives can evolve to tackle not just community development but also social justice.

"A Prisoner of Injustice" concludes with Thabo being released on bail, thanks to the relentless efforts of his legal team and the public support he receives. His release is a bittersweet moment.

While he is elated to be reunited with his family and community, he is acutely aware of the challenges that lie ahead in clearing his name and rebuilding his life's work.

The chapter ends with Thabo stepping out of the prison gates, greeted by a crowd of supporters. This moment is not just a personal victory; it symbolizes a renewed commitment to his mission and a deepened understanding of the injustices that pervade society. Thabo's journey has taken on a new dimension, one that encompasses a broader fight for justice and equity.

As Thabo Mokoena endures the challenges of his imprisonment in "A Prisoner of Injustice," he faces a period of deep reflection and transformation. The chapter continues to delve into his journey, exploring themes of resilience, growth, and the fight for justice from within the confines of his cell.

Locked away from the community he has dedicated his life to serving, Thabo finds himself confronting the harsh realities of the justice system. His days are marked by a monotonous routine, starkly contrasting with the dynamic and purpose-driven life he once led. Yet, even within these walls, Thabo's spirit of service and leadership does not wane.

Amidst the despair, Thabo becomes a source of support and guidance for his fellow inmates. He listens to their stories, many of which echo his own experiences of injustice and wrongful accusation. These interactions are eye-opening, exposing Thabo to the myriad ways in which the justice system can fail those it's meant to protect.

During this time, Thabo's thoughts often turn to his community projects and the soccer team. He worries about their sustainability in his absence and the impact his situation might have on the youth he has mentored. These concerns are a constant reminder of the stakes of his legal battle.

Meanwhile, outside the prison, the community's support for Thabo grows stronger. Rallies and campaigns calling for his release are organized, drawing attention to his case and the broader issues of judicial fairness. The soccer team plays a crucial role in these efforts, using their matches as platforms to advocate for Thabo's cause.

As the legal proceedings continue, Thabo's lawyers uncover key evidence and witness testimonies that challenge the basis of his imprisonment. These developments offer a glimmer of hope, suggesting that Thabo's fight for justice might soon yield positive results.

The chapter also explores the emotional toll on Thabo's family. They grapple with the public scrutiny and the personal pain of seeing Thabo behind bars. Despite these challenges, their resolve to support him remains unshaken, providing Thabo with a vital emotional anchor.

"A Prisoner of Injustice" concludes with a pivotal court hearing. The new evidence presented by Thabo's legal team leads to a re-evaluation of his case. The chapter ends on a cliff-hanger, with the judge about to deliver a verdict that has the potential to change Thabo's fate. This moment is laden with anticipation, not just for Thabo but for the entire community that has rallied behind him.

The chapter is a profound exploration of the human spirit's resilience in the face of adversity and the importance of community solidarity in battling injustice. Thabo's story becomes a beacon of hope and a testament to the enduring fight for fairness and truth.

LIBERATION AND LOSS

Liberation and Loss, Thabo Mokoena's journey takes a pivotal turn as he confronts the outcomes of his legal battle and the personal and communal repercussions of his incarceration.

The chapter opens in the tense moments of the courtroom, with the judge ready to deliver the verdict. The air is thick with anticipation. Thabo stands, surrounded by his legal team, family, and a contingent of community supporters who have come to witness this crucial moment.

The judge announces Thabo's acquittal, citing the new evidence and testimonies that have shed light on the injustices he faced. The courtroom erupts in a mixture of relief and jubilation. Thabo's release is not just a personal victory; it symbolizes a triumph for the community and for all those who have supported him through this ordeal.

However, Thabo's liberation from prison is bittersweet. He steps back into a world that has moved on in his absence. The community projects and the soccer team, though sustained by dedicated individuals, have faced setbacks and challenges without his leadership. Thabo realizes the road to rebuilding will be arduous.

The narrative then delves into Thabo's emotional state. Despite his relief at being exonerated, he grapples with a sense of loss – loss of time, opportunities, and, in some ways, his sense of identity. His imprisonment has changed him, deepening his understanding of societal injustices and the fragility of progress.

Thabo also faces the daunting task of mending strained relationships, both personal and professional. His family, though overjoyed at his return, has been deeply affected by the ordeal. There are moments of tension and unspoken grievances that Thabo works to address, recognizing the emotional toll his absence has taken on his loved ones.

In the community, Thabo's return is met with a mixture of reactions. While many celebrate his release and welcome him back with open arms, others remain sceptical, their trust eroded by the allegations and the media frenzy. Thabo approaches these challenges with humility, seeking to rebuild bridges and restore confidence in his leadership.

As Thabo begins to reengage with his community work, he finds that his perspective has shifted. His experience in prison has given him a deeper insight into the systemic issues facing marginalized communities. He starts to integrate these insights into his projects, focusing not just on community development but also on advocacy and social justice.

The chapter concludes with Thabo organizing a community gathering, where he shares his experiences and his renewed vision for their collective future. It's a moment of reflection and reconnection, marking the beginning of a new chapter in Thabo's journey.

"Liberation and Loss" is a poignant exploration of the complexities of returning to normalcy after a profound personal upheaval. It highlights Thabo's resilience, the enduring support of his community, and the transformative power of adversity. The chapter sets the stage for Thabo's continued quest to effect change and address the deeper systemic issues he has come to understand more intimately.

As "Liberation and Loss" continues, Thabo Mokoena's journey takes on a renewed sense of purpose, tempered by the realities and insights gained from his incarceration.

In the aftermath of the community gathering, Thabo finds himself at a crossroads. The landscape of his initiatives has shifted, and he recognizes the need for a new approach. He spends time reconnecting with the leaders of his various projects, assessing the changes and challenges that have arisen in his absence. Thabo's approach is more collaborative now; he is keenly aware of the value of diverse perspectives and shared leadership.

The soccer team, a source of great pride and unity for the community, has faced its struggles but remains a beacon of hope. Thabo reconnects with the players, their shared experiences fostering a deeper bond. He finds joy and inspiration in their resilience, which in turn fuels his passion for the project.

However, the path to rebuilding is fraught with challenges. Thabo encounters scepticism from some community members and local leaders. The scars of the allegations and the trial linger, affecting people's perceptions and trust. Thabo understands these sentiments; he approaches these challenges with patience, focusing on consistent and transparent actions to rebuild trust.

Amidst this, Thabo grapples with a personal sense of loss. His time in prison has taken a toll on his personal relationships and his sense of self. He undergoes periods of introspection, where he questions his decisions and the sacrifices he has made. These moments are difficult, but they also provide Thabo with a deeper understanding of himself and his mission.

Thabo's journey of rebuilding extends beyond the tangible aspects of his projects. He starts to advocate for criminal justice reform, drawing from his experiences to highlight the systemic issues within the justice system. He engages in public speaking, participates in forums, and collaborates with advocacy groups, using his story to push for change.

The narrative then shifts to a small yet significant victory in Thabo's efforts to rejuvenate his community projects. A major event organized by the tech incubator receives widespread support and media attention, signalling a turning point in the community's perception of Thabo's initiatives. The success of the event is a testament to the resilience and potential of the community, and it reignites a sense of hope and possibility.

As "Liberation and Loss" concludes, Thabo reflects on the journey that has brought him to this point. He recognizes that his path will always be one of both challenges and triumphs. Yet, he remains committed to his mission, driven by a deeper understanding of the complexities of social change and the unyielding spirit of his community.

The chapter ends with Thabo looking out over a community gathering, a scene reminiscent of his earlier days. The sense of loss he feels is intertwined with a sense of gratitude and a renewed commitment to his life's work. "Liberation and Loss" thus becomes not just a story of personal struggle, but a narrative of enduring hope and the unbreakable resolve to continue making a difference.

REBIRTH UNDER A NEW NAME

Rebirth Under a New Name, Thabo Mokoena embarks on a transformative journey, reinventing himself and his initiatives to better serve his community and address the broader societal issues he has come to understand more deeply.

The chapter begins with Thabo making a symbolic yet significant decision: he rebrands his community projects and the soccer team. This rebranding is more than just a change of name; it represents a new direction and a renewed commitment to his mission. The new names reflect the lessons learned from his challenges and his vision for the future.

Thabo's first step in this rebirth is to revitalize the soccer team. He recognizes the team's potential to inspire and unite the community. The rebranded team, with a new name and logo, becomes a symbol of resilience and hope. Thabo works tirelessly to secure new sponsorships, rebuild the team's infrastructure, and introduce youth development programs that focus on both sports and education.

In parallel, Thabo reimagines his community development initiatives. Drawing from his experiences and the insights gained during his incarceration, he expands the scope of his projects to include advocacy on social justice issues.

He establishes partnerships with local and national organizations to address systemic challenges such as access to education, healthcare, and criminal justice reform.

A significant part of the chapter is dedicated to the launch of Thabo's new flagship project: a community centre that serves as a hub for various initiatives. This centre offers educational programs, vocational training, health services, and legal aid. It becomes a beacon of community empowerment and a place where individuals can find support, learn new skills, and work towards a better future.

Thabo also reengages with the tech incubator, infusing it with a renewed sense of purpose. He mentors young entrepreneurs, focusing not just on technological innovation but also on social entrepreneurship. The incubator becomes a space where technology meets societal needs, fostering innovations that aim to improve the quality of life in the community and beyond.

The narrative then explores Thabo's personal transformation. He adopts a more reflective and inclusive leadership style, shaped by the trials he has faced. Thabo's experiences have deepened his empathy and understanding of the complexities of social change. He becomes more open to listening and learning from others, recognizing that true leadership involves empowering those around him.

As "Rebirth Under a New Name" concludes, Thabo organizes a community celebration to officially launch the new initiatives. The event is a vibrant affair, attended by community members, local leaders, and representatives from various organizations. It's a moment of joy and pride, marking the beginning of a new chapter in Thabo's journey and the community's journey.

The chapter ends with Thabo delivering a speech at the event, where he reflects on the past and looks forward to the future. He talks about the power of resilience, the importance of community, and the potential for change. "Rebirth Under a New Name" is a testament to Thabo's unwavering commitment to his community, his ability to adapt and grow, and his enduring vision for a better future.

As "Rebirth Under a New Name" continues, Thabo Mokoena's journey of transformation and renewal unfolds, revealing the impact of his reinvigorated efforts on the community and beyond.

The chapter further explores the various initiatives birthed from the community centre. One key program that gains attention is a youth mentorship program, where experienced members of the community, including Thabo himself, guide young individuals in personal and professional development. This program not only nurtures future leaders but also strengthens the community's social fabric.

Another highlight is the establishment of a health and wellness initiative within the community centre, addressing a crucial need that Thabo identified during his interactions with the community. This program offers health education, basic medical services, and wellness activities, significantly improving the community's overall health and well-being.

Thabo's renewed focus on social entrepreneurship leads to the creation of several small businesses and start-ups, emerging from the incubator program. These ventures are community-oriented, addressing local needs such as sustainable agriculture, renewable energy, and digital literacy. Thabo's guidance ensures that these enterprises maintain a balance between profitability and social impact.

The rebranded soccer team, embodying the spirit of the community's resurgence, begins to climb the ranks in local and regional leagues. Their success on the field brings joy and pride to the community, serving as a testament to their hard work and Thabo's renewed leadership. The team also engages in community outreach, participating in educational and social campaigns, further solidifying their role as community ambassadors.

As the narrative progresses, Thabo's personal evolution becomes evident. He is more reflective, grounded, and open to collaboration. His experiences have taught him the value of resilience, not just as a means to overcome challenges but as a vital component of sustainable community development.

Thabo also becomes a more vocal advocate for social justice, drawing from his own experiences to highlight broader societal issues. He participates in forums and discussions, bringing attention to the need for systemic change and the importance of community-based solutions.

The chapter concludes with a reflective Thabo looking over the community centre, bustling with activity and life. He realizes that his journey has come full circle. The struggles and challenges he faced have not only transformed him but also deepened his commitment to his community. He sees the tangible results of his work in the lives of those around him and in the vibrant energy of the community.

"Rebirth Under a New Name" ends with a sense of fulfilment and anticipation. Thabo understands that his journey will continue to evolve, with new challenges and opportunities. Yet, he remains dedicated to his mission, empowered by the resilience and spirit of his community, and driven by a vision that extends beyond himself to the betterment of society as a whole.

QUIET STEPS TO RECOVERY

Quiet Steps to Recovery, Thabo Mokoena embarks on a more introspective and measured phase of his journey. This chapter focuses on the gradual process of healing and rebuilding, both for Thabo personally and for the community projects that have endured through turbulent times.

The chapter opens with Thabo taking time for personal reflection. The trials he has faced have left indelible marks, and he recognizes the need for a period of healing and self-care. He engages in quieter activities that foster personal growth and well-being, such as spending time in nature, meditating, and reconnecting with old hobbies that had been set aside in his busier days.

Simultaneously, Thabo takes a step back from being the forefront leader of his community projects, transitioning into a more advisory role. This change allows for new leaders within the community to emerge and take the reins, fostering a sense of empowerment and sustainability within the initiatives.

One key aspect of this chapter is Thabo's focus on strengthening the resilience of his community projects. He implements systems and structures that ensure these initiatives can withstand future challenges without relying solely on his leadership.

This process involves extensive training programs for emerging leaders, establishing strong governance frameworks, and fostering a culture of collective responsibility.

The soccer team, which has been a central part of Thabo's journey, also undergoes a transformation. Thabo works with the coaching staff to develop a program that emphasizes not just athletic excellence but also personal development and community service. The team becomes more than just a sports entity; it evolves into a holistic development program for the youth.

In the community, Thabo's quieter presence is felt differently but no less significantly. He participates in community events and gatherings, not as a speaker or organizer, but as a listener and supporter. This approach allows him to reconnect with the community members on a more personal level, understanding their evolving needs and aspirations.

Thabo's legal battles and the challenges he faced also inspire him to advocate for broader systemic changes. He collaborates with legal experts and social activists to campaign for reforms in the justice system, drawing on his experiences to highlight the need for fairness and transparency.

As "Quiet Steps to Recovery" draws to a close, Thabo reflects on the evolution of his journey. He finds a new sense of balance in his life, integrating his passion for community service with the need for personal well-being and growth. The chapter ends with Thabo at a community celebration, observing the joy and unity of the people he has served. He realizes that true recovery and resilience lie in the strength of the community and the collective spirit of hope and perseverance.

"Quiet Steps to Recovery" is a testament to the power of quiet reflection, the importance of self-care in leadership, and the enduring impact of empowering others. It marks a period of healing and growth, setting a foundation for a sustainable and resilient future for Thabo and the community he cherishes.

As "Quiet Steps to Recovery" progresses, Thabo Mokoena's journey of healing and growth deepens, reflecting a more nuanced understanding of leadership and community development.

The narrative delves into Thabo's efforts to nurture the new leadership emerging within his community projects. He adopts a mentorship role, providing guidance and support while allowing these new leaders to bring their ideas and energy to the forefront. This shift not only invigorates the projects with fresh perspectives but also ensures their longevity and resilience.

Thabo's personal journey of recovery is marked by moments of introspection. He spends time reconnecting with his cultural roots, drawing strength and wisdom from traditions and practices that he had lost touch with in his years of relentless work. This reconnection brings him a sense of peace and grounding, reinforcing his identity and purpose.

In his advisory role, Thabo focuses on building partnerships that extend beyond the immediate community. He engages with regional and national organizations, leveraging these relationships to bring more resources and opportunities to his community. These partnerships lead to the development of new programs that address issues such as environmental sustainability, digital inclusion, and economic empowerment.

The soccer team, under the new leadership, continues to be a source of pride for the community. The players, inspired by Thabo's example, become more involved in community service and mentoring younger players. The team's success on the field is now matched by their impact off the field, embodying the principles of teamwork, discipline, and social responsibility.

Thabo also revisits the tech incubator, which has evolved under the guidance of the young entrepreneurs he mentored. The incubator now serves as a hub for innovation, not just in technology but also in social enterprise.

It becomes a model for other communities, demonstrating how technology can be harnessed to address social challenges and improve lives.

Throughout the chapter, Thabo's interactions with the community reflect a quieter, more reflective approach. He listens more than he speaks, learning from the experiences and insights of community members. These interactions are not only healing for Thabo but also affirm the community's respect and appreciation for his enduring commitment.

As "Quiet Steps to Recovery" concludes, Thabo finds himself at a community gathering, watching a group of children play in a field he helped to develop. He reflects on the journey that has brought him here – the successes, the setbacks, and the lessons learned. The chapter ends with Thabo acknowledging that while his path has changed, his dedication to his community remains unwavering.

"Quiet Steps to Recovery" is a chapter about the transformative power of resilience, the importance of community in personal healing, and the value of empowering others to lead. It closes with a sense of hope and a reaffirmation of Thabo's commitment to his community's ongoing journey towards a better, more inclusive future.

REBUILDING IN THE SHADOWS

Rebuilding in the Shadows, Thabo Mokoena embarks on a less visible yet impactful phase of his journey. This chapter explores the concept of leadership from behind the scenes and the subtle yet profound ways in which Thabo contributes to his community's resurgence.

The chapter begins with Thabo deliberately stepping away from the limelight. After the trials and tribulations, he has faced, he chooses a more understated approach to his involvement in community projects. This decision is not born out of fear or defeat but from a deep understanding that true empowerment comes when the community takes charge of its destiny.

Thabo focuses on supporting the infrastructure of the community initiatives from the background. He leverages his experience and connections to secure funding, provide strategic advice, and facilitate partnerships, all while ensuring that the community leaders are at the forefront.

A significant aspect of "Rebuilding in the Shadows" is Thabo's work with the youth. He believes that nurturing the next generation is crucial for sustainable change. Thabo sets up workshops and mentorship programs, focusing on leadership development, critical thinking, and civic responsibility. His interactions with the youth are more personal and reflective, as he shares the lessons learned from his journey.

The narrative then explores the ongoing evolution of the community centre. Under the new leadership, supported by Thabo's guidance, the centre expands its offerings. It becomes a hub for cultural activities, educational programs, and start-up incubation, reflecting the diverse needs and aspirations of the community.

Thabo also plays a key role in establishing a community fund. This fund, financed through local contributions and external donations, provides resources for small community-led projects. It's a testament to the community's resilience and self-sufficiency, values that Thabo has always championed.

Throughout the chapter, Thabo grapples with his role in the shadows. He reflects on the changes in his approach to leadership and service. There are moments of doubt, where he wonders if he is making a difference. Yet, these moments are countered by the tangible impacts of his behind-the-scenes work.

As "Rebuilding in the Shadows" draws to a close, Thabo attends a community festival organized by the leaders he has mentored. He watches from the side-lines as the community celebrates its culture, achievements, and unity. The success of the festival and the vibrancy of the community are affirmations of the effectiveness of his new role.

Thabo in quiet contemplation, satisfied with the knowledge that his contributions, though less visible, are deeply felt. "Rebuilding in the Shadows" is a powerful exploration of humility in leadership, the strength of community-driven change, and the enduring impact of supporting others to lead. It sets a tone of quiet optimism and reaffirms Thabo's commitment to serving his community, regardless of where he stands.

As "Rebuilding in the Shadows" continues, Thabo Mokoena's journey of quiet contribution and behind-the-scenes support further cements his legacy as a catalyst for community empowerment and growth.

Thabo's new approach leads him to explore collaborations that were previously untapped. He reaches out to local and regional organizations, advocating for programs that benefit his community. Thabo's expertise and experience become invaluable in these collaborations, enabling him to secure resources and opportunities that are directly funnelled into community projects.

The narrative then shifts to focus on a significant initiative that Thabo quietly spearheads: a community-based environmental sustainability program. Recognizing the importance of environmental stewardship, Thabo works with local leaders to develop initiatives that promote sustainable practices, such as community gardens, waste recycling programs, and renewable energy projects.

These initiatives not only contribute to environmental health but also create job opportunities and foster a sense of communal responsibility. In his role as a mentor, Thabo continues to engage with the youth, but now his focus is on fostering critical thinking and problem-solving skills.

He organizes workshops and discussion groups where young people are encouraged to analyse community challenges and develop innovative solutions. Thabo's role in these sessions is less of an instructor and more of a facilitator, guiding the conversation while allowing the youth to take the lead.

A poignant moment in the chapter occurs during a visit to the soccer team. Thabo observes a match from the side-lines, witnessing the team's growth and the positive influence they have on the younger players. The team's success on the field is mirrored by their role as community leaders, a testament to the enduring impact of Thabo's vision and mentorship.

As Thabo continues his work, he remains mindful of the importance of self-care and balance. He finds solace in quieter moments, whether it's a walk-in nature or time spent with family and friends. These moments of reflection and connection are crucial, providing him with the strength and perspective needed to continue his work.

The chapter concludes with Thabo attending a community meeting where various projects and initiatives are showcased. Thabo listens with pride as community members present their achievements and plans for the future.

It's a moment that encapsulates the essence of his work in the shadows – empowering others to lead and create positive change.

"Rebuilding in the Shadows" ends with Thabo looking on at the thriving community, a quiet smile on his face. His journey has shown that leadership doesn't always require being in the spotlight; sometimes, the greatest impact can be made from the side-lines, nurturing and supporting others to shine. The chapter closes with a sense of fulfilment and hope, as Thabo's legacy lives on in the empowered community and the leaders he has helped to cultivate.

THE DAWN OF DEMOCRACY

The Dawn of Democracy, Thabo Mokoena's journey intertwines with a pivotal moment in his nation's history. The chapter explores how the shift towards a democratic society impacts Thabo's community work and the broader context in which he operates.

The chapter begins on the eve of a historic election, the first in which all citizens, regardless of race, are allowed to vote. This momentous occasion marks a significant shift in the political landscape and brings a wave of hope and anticipation across the nation, including in Thabo's community.

Thabo, witnessing the dawn of this new era, feels a renewed sense of purpose. The political changes open up new possibilities for addressing the systemic issues that have long plagued his community. He sees this as an opportunity to advocate for policies and programs that can bring about meaningful change at a larger scale.

The narrative then explores Thabo's role in the transitioning period. He becomes actively involved in civic education, helping to inform his community about their rights and the importance of their vote. Thabo organizes workshops and discussion forums, ensuring that the community is not just aware of the political changes but also engaged and empowered to participate in the democratic process.

As the nation undergoes this transformation, Thabo revisits his community projects with a new perspective. He aligns his initiatives with the broader national agenda of building a more inclusive and equitable society. This alignment leads to new partnerships with government agencies and non-governmental organizations, enhancing the scope and impact of his work.

One significant development in this chapter is the increased support for Thabo's community centre. The centre becomes a focal point for democratic engagement, hosting political debates, voter registration drives, and leadership training sessions. It evolves into a space where democracy is not just discussed but actively practiced and nurtured.

Thabo also witnesses the impact of the democratic transition on the soccer team. The team, which has always been a source of community pride, now also becomes a symbol of national unity and hope. The players, inspired by the changing times, engage more actively in social issues, using their platform to promote peace, unity, and democratic values.

The chapter concludes with Thabo reflecting on the changes around him. He attends the historic election, casting his vote with a sense of pride and optimism. The chapter ends with Thabo amidst a crowd of fellow citizens, celebrating the birth of a new era. It's a moment of collective triumph, a culmination of the struggles and hopes of a nation.

"The Dawn of Democracy" is a chapter about the intersection of community action and national transformation. It highlights Thabo's ability to adapt his work to the changing political landscape and his continued commitment to leveraging these changes for the betterment of his community. The chapter closes with a sense of optimism and a look towards a future filled with possibilities for Thabo and his nation.

As "The Dawn of Democracy" progresses, Thabo Mokoena's journey becomes increasingly intertwined with the nation's journey towards a new democratic reality. The chapter continues to explore how this significant political shift shapes Thabo's community involvement and advocacy work.

Following the election, the atmosphere in Thabo's community is one of cautious optimism. There is a palpable sense of excitement about the possibilities that democracy brings, but also an awareness of the challenges that lie ahead in addressing the legacies of inequality and injustice.

Thabo seizes this moment to amplify his efforts in community development. With the changing political landscape, he finds new avenues to advocate for his community at a policy level. He engages with newly elected officials, many of whom are receptive to grassroots perspectives. Thabo works to ensure that the voices and needs of his community are considered in the shaping of new policies and programs.

The narrative then shifts to highlight a series of community dialogues that Thabo organizes. These dialogues are platforms for residents to discuss their aspirations and concerns in the new democratic context. They also serve as a space for civic education, where community members learn about their rights, the importance of civic participation, and ways to hold their elected representatives accountable.

In these dialogues, Thabo emphasizes the importance of active citizenship and community solidarity in shaping the future of their democracy. He encourages the community to view the democratic transition not just as a change in political leadership, but as an opportunity to redefine their societal values and work towards a more inclusive and equitable community.

A significant development in the chapter is Thabo's initiative to create a community-led development plan. This plan, developed through a series of participatory workshops, outlines the community's priorities and strategies for development in the new democratic era. It becomes a guiding document for Thabo's initiatives and a model for other communities.

Thabo also revisits the soccer team, which has grown into more than just a sports club under his guidance. The team becomes actively involved in promoting democratic values and civic engagement among the youth.

Players participate in community service projects, voter education campaigns, and peace-building activities, symbolizing the role of sports in fostering unity and social responsibility.

As the chapter concludes, Thabo stands at a community festival celebrating the first anniversary of the historic election. He looks around at the faces of his fellow community members, filled with hope and determination. The chapter ends with Thabo delivering a speech, where he reflects on the journey of his community and the nation. He speaks of the challenges they have overcome and the work that still lies ahead in building a truly inclusive democracy.

"The Dawn of Democracy" closes with a sense of achievement and a forward-looking perspective. It underscores Thabo's role in bridging community action and national development, highlighting his enduring commitment to leveraging democratic change for the betterment of his community and country. The chapter sets the stage for continued growth and engagement in a nation reborn with democratic ideals.

NAVIGATING A NEW SOUTH AFRICA

Navigating a New South Africa, Thabo Mokoena's journey evolves as he and his community adjust to the realities and challenges of a post-apartheid society. This chapter explores the complexities of transition and Thabo's role in guiding his community through the nuances of this new era.

The chapter opens with Thabo reflecting on the changes that the democratic transition has brought. While there is a sense of liberation and hope, there are also significant challenges. Inequalities and social divisions persist, and the expectations of rapid transformation are met with the realities of slow systemic change.

Thabo recognizes that his community's journey is reflective of the broader national experience. He sees the need for patience, perseverance, and continuous effort to address the deep-seated issues that decades of inequality have entrenched. Thabo begins to focus on long-term strategies for sustainable development, rather than seeking immediate solutions.

A key aspect of this chapter is Thabo's engagement with new governmental structures and policies. He becomes an intermediary between his community and the government, helping to navigate the bureaucracy and advocate for resources and support.

Thabo works to build constructive relationships with local and national leaders, ensuring that his community has a voice in the new South Africa.

The narrative then explores the evolution of Thabo's community projects in the context of the new political landscape. He adapts his initiatives to align with national development goals, focusing on areas such as education reform, economic empowerment, and social cohesion. Thabo's projects become models of community-led development, demonstrating the potential of grassroots initiatives to complement government efforts.

Thabo also faces the challenge of managing expectations within his community. The euphoria of the democratic transition has given way to a realization that change is a gradual process. Thabo addresses this by fostering a culture of realistic optimism, encouraging the community to celebrate the progress made while acknowledging the work that still needs to be done.

Another significant development in the chapter is Thabo's effort to address the lingering wounds of apartheid within his community. He organizes reconciliation forums and cultural exchange programs, promoting understanding and healing among different community groups. These initiatives help to bridge divides and foster a sense of unity in the diverse community.

As "Navigating a New South Africa" draws to a close, Thabo finds himself at a community event celebrating a national holiday. He observes the festivities, a blend of cultural expressions and a testament to the nation's diversity and resilience. The chapter concludes with Thabo delivering a speech that encapsulates his journey and the journey of his nation. He speaks of the challenges faced, the milestones achieved, and the enduring spirit of hope and determination that drives them forward.

"Navigating a New South Africa" is a reflection of Thabo's growth as a leader and the community's evolution in a changing nation. It highlights the importance of adaptability, patience, and sustained effort in building a society that honours its past while striving towards a more equitable and united future.

As "Navigating a New South Africa" continues, Thabo Mokoena's role in his evolving nation takes on new dimensions, reflecting the complexities and opportunities of this era of change.

Thabo becomes increasingly involved in initiatives that bridge the gap between government policies and grassroots needs. Recognizing that true change requires collaboration across different sectors, he facilitates partnerships between community groups, government agencies, and private organizations. These collaborations aim to create integrated solutions for issues such as housing, employment, and education.

The narrative then shifts to highlight a new challenge facing Thabo and his community: the surge of urbanization. As more people migrate to cities in search of better opportunities, Thabo works to ensure that his community does not get left behind in the rapid development. He advocates for inclusive urban planning policies and initiates local development projects that are sustainable and community-cantered.

In this new South Africa, Thabo also witnesses the rise of a new generation – young people who have grown up in a post-apartheid era. He sees immense potential in these youth and dedicates efforts to engage and empower them. Thabo organizes leadership workshops and forums where young voices can be heard and nurtured. He believes that these young individuals are not just future leaders but also key players in the current narrative of the nation.

One of the key developments in the chapter is the establishment of a cultural exchange program initiated by Thabo. This program brings together people from diverse backgrounds within South Africa to share their experiences and cultures. It becomes a powerful tool for promoting understanding and unity in a country still grappling with its divided past.

Thabo's approach to his community work also evolves. He focuses on creating self-sustaining initiatives that can continue without his direct involvement, ensuring the longevity and independence of the projects. He mentors a new set of community leaders, imparting the skills and knowledge they need to take over the helm of various initiatives.

As the chapter nears its end, Thabo reflects on the journey of his nation and his role in it. He attends a national conference on community development, where he is recognized for his contributions. The recognition is a testament to Thabo's impact, but for him, the true reward is seeing his community thrive and adapt in a new South Africa.

"Navigating a New South Africa" concludes with Thabo looking ahead, aware of the challenges that remain but optimistic about the future. He understands that the path to a just and equitable society is long and complex, but he remains committed to playing his part in it. The chapter closes with a sense of hope and determination, as Thabo and his community continue to navigate the ever-changing landscape of their nation.

A NEW ERA FOR BUSINESS

A New Era for Business, Thabo Mokoena shifts his focus to the economic landscape of the new South Africa, exploring the opportunities and challenges that come with the nation's evolving business environment. This chapter delves into Thabo's efforts to foster economic development and entrepreneurship within his community in the context of a changing economy.

The chapter opens with Thabo assessing the economic shifts occurring in post-apartheid South Africa. He notices the rise of new industries and the increasing importance of technology and innovation in the business world. Thabo sees these changes as an opportunity to drive economic growth and empowerment within his community.

Thabo's first step in this new venture is to revitalize the tech incubator he established earlier. He upgrades the facility with modern technology and resources, turning it into a hub for aspiring entrepreneurs and innovators. Thabo partners with business schools, technology companies, and investors to provide mentorship, training, and funding opportunities for the incubator participants.

The narrative then explores Thabo's initiatives to promote small and medium-sized enterprises (SMEs) in the community.

He organizes business development workshops and establishes a microfinance program to provide capital to local entrepreneurs. These efforts aim to stimulate local economic growth and create job opportunities.

One of the key aspects of this chapter is Thabo's emphasis on sustainable and socially responsible business practices. He encourages entrepreneurs to develop businesses that not only are profitable but also contribute positively to the community. This approach leads to the emergence of enterprises focused on renewable energy, waste management, and community health initiatives.

Thabo also faces challenges in this new endeavour. He navigates the complexities of the business world, including competition, regulatory hurdles, and the need for market access. Thabo works to build networks and alliances that can help overcome these challenges and provide support to the burgeoning local businesses.

A significant development in the chapter is the launch of a community marketplace, a platform for local entrepreneurs to showcase and sell their products and services. This marketplace becomes a symbol of the community's entrepreneurial spirit and its potential to contribute to the broader economy.

As "A New Era for Business" draws to a close, Thabo reflects on the progress made. He attends a community fair where local businesses and start-ups display their innovations. The fair is not just a celebration of entrepreneurial success; it's a testament to the community's ability to adapt and thrive in a changing economic landscape.

Thabo looking at the bustling fair, filled with a sense of accomplishment and hope. "A New Era for Business" is a chapter about embracing change, fostering economic empowerment, and the role of business in building a more prosperous and equitable society. It underscores Thabo's belief in the power of entrepreneurship to drive social and economic change, marking a new chapter in his journey of community development.

As "A New Era for Business" progresses, Thabo Mokoena's role as a community leader and business mentor grows increasingly significant in guiding the economic transformation of his community in a rapidly evolving South Africa.

The narrative delves deeper into Thabo's efforts to integrate his community into the broader national economy. Recognizing the potential of the digital economy, Thabo focuses on digital literacy and technology training programs. He understands that equipping the youth and entrepreneurs with digital skills is crucial for their competitiveness in the modern marketplace.

Thabo also identifies the need for market access for local businesses. He establishes partnerships with larger corporations and government agencies to create channels for local products and services to reach wider markets. These partnerships prove to be mutually beneficial, offering larger entities access to local innovation and talent, while providing the community with growth opportunities.

A significant theme in this chapter is Thabo's emphasis on innovation and creativity in business. He organizes innovation challenges and hackathons, encouraging community members, especially the youth, to come up with solutions to local problems. These events not only foster a culture of innovation but also attract attention and support from tech companies and investors.

The narrative then shifts to a story of success. One of the start-ups from Thabo's incubator, focusing on sustainable agriculture, gains national recognition. This success story becomes an inspiration for the community, demonstrating the potential of local entrepreneurs to make an impact at a national level.

In the midst of these developments, Thabo faces the challenge of balancing growth with sustainability. He advocates for responsible business practices and ensures that the economic growth within the community does not come at the cost of environmental degradation or social disparity. Thabo's leadership in this regard sets a precedent for ethical and sustainable business practices in the community.

As "A New Era for Business" nears its conclusion, Thabo organizes a community summit that brings together local entrepreneurs, investors, government representatives, and members of the community. The summit is a platform for dialogue, networking, and showcasing the community's achievements in business and innovation.

Thabo delivering a speech at the summit, reflecting on the journey of the community in adapting to the new economic landscape. He talks about the importance of resilience, innovation, and collaboration in creating a prosperous and inclusive economy.

"A New Era for Business" ends with a sense of achievement and optimism. Thabo's initiatives have not only sparked economic growth in his community but have also empowered its members to be active participants in the nation's economy. The chapter closes with Thabo looking forward to the future, ready to tackle the next set of challenges and opportunities in the evolving business world of South Africa.

As "A New Era for Business" further unfolds, Thabo Mokoena's initiatives continue to intersect with the broader economic transformation of South Africa, showcasing the dynamic role of grassroots leadership in shaping a nation's economic landscape.

Thabo's focus on creating a supportive ecosystem for entrepreneurs leads to the establishment of a series of workshops and seminars aimed at skill development and business acumen.

He collaborates with experts in various fields – finance, marketing, technology – to provide comprehensive training for aspiring entrepreneurs. These workshops become a cornerstone for many local businesses, equipping them with the tools needed to thrive in a competitive market.

Another significant development in the chapter is Thabo's initiative to bridge the digital divide. He recognizes that access to technology is a critical factor in business success. To address this, Thabo launches a program to provide affordable internet access and digital devices to the community, particularly targeting young entrepreneurs and students. This program significantly enhances the community's ability to engage with the digital economy, opening up new opportunities and avenues for growth.

Thabo also begins to explore international markets as a potential avenue for the community's products and services. He understands the value of global exposure and works to establish connections with international partners and networks. These efforts lead to some local businesses expanding their reach beyond South Africa, showcasing the quality and innovation of their products and services on a global stage.

In the midst of these successes, Thabo remains vigilant about the challenges of rapid growth. He emphasizes the importance of sustainable and ethical business practices, ensuring that economic development does not come at the expense of social and environmental responsibility. This focus leads to the integration of sustainable practices in all of Thabo's community projects, setting a standard for responsible business in the community.

The narrative then shifts to a moment of recognition for Thabo's efforts. He is invited to speak at a national conference on economic development, where he shares his insights and experiences in fostering community-based entrepreneurship. Thabo's speech is well-received, highlighting his role as a thought leader in the field of community-driven economic development.

As "A New Era for Business" concludes, a sense of pride and accomplishment is evident in Thabo's community. The local businesses and start-ups nurtured under Thabo's guidance are not only contributing to the community's economic vitality but are also serving as examples of the potential inherent in grassroots initiatives.

The chapter ends with Thabo reflecting on the journey thus far. He realizes that while there is still much to be done, the strides made in empowering his community economically have laid a strong foundation for future growth and prosperity. "A New Era for Business" closes with Thabo reaffirmed in his belief that economic empowerment is key to lasting social change, and his commitment to this cause remains unwavering as he looks to the future.

UNSEEN INFLUENCE

Unseen Influence, Thabo Mokoena's journey takes a turn towards the subtle yet impactful ways he shapes his community and inspires change without being in the direct spotlight. This chapter explores the concept of influence that extends beyond visible leadership and the profound impact it can have.

The chapter begins with Thabo taking a step back from public-facing roles in his various initiatives. He transitions into a role that is more about guidance and less about direct management. This change is not a retreat but a strategic shift to empower others to take leadership positions.

Thabo's focus shifts to mentoring emerging leaders in his community. He spends time with individuals who show potential in various fields – from business to social work to politics. Thabo shares his experiences, offering advice and insights, but more importantly, he listens and learns from these future leaders, understanding their visions and challenges.

A significant aspect of this chapter is Thabo's behind-the-scenes work in influencing policy and decision-making. Using the network and respect he has built over the years; Thabo engages with local and national leaders to advocate for policies that benefit his community.

His influence is subtle but effective, as he works to ensure that the voices and needs of his community are considered in larger conversations.

The narrative then explores the ripple effect of Thabo's mentorship and advocacy. Stories emerge of individuals and groups within the community who, inspired by Thabo's guidance, initiate their projects and advocacy efforts. These initiatives range from environmental campaigns to educational programs, each reflecting the values and lessons imparted by Thabo.

Thabo's unseen influence extends to the cultural fabric of the community. He supports arts and cultural programs that celebrate and preserve the community's heritage. These programs not only enrich the cultural life of the community but also foster a sense of identity and pride.

A poignant moment in the chapter is when Thabo attends a community event where several projects he influenced are showcased. He watches from the background, seeing the seeds he planted bearing fruit. The success of these projects is not credited to him directly, but his role in nurturing them is recognized by those who know him.

As "Unseen Influence" draws to a close, Thabo reflects on this phase of his journey. He finds satisfaction in the knowledge that his impact is woven into the fabric of the community in ways that are not always visible but are deeply felt. He understands that true influence often lies in empowering others to find their paths and make their mark.

Thabo looking over a vibrant community, teeming with initiatives and leaders that he helped to cultivate. "Unseen Influence" is a testament to the power of mentorship, advocacy, and the impact of leading from behind. It closes with a sense of fulfilment and the acknowledgment that Thabo's legacy will live on through the lives and actions of those he has inspired and guided.

As "Unseen Influence" continues, Thabo Mokoena's subtle yet profound impact on his community unfolds further, showcasing the enduring power of mentorship and the ripple effects of thoughtful, behind-the-scenes action.

The chapter delves deeper into the various ways Thabo's mentorship manifests in the community. One of the key highlights is the growth of a youth leadership program that Thabo helped to initiate. This program, now run entirely by local young leaders, is making significant strides in engaging and empowering the youth. The program not only focuses on leadership skills but also encourages active citizenship and community service.

Thabo also plays a crucial role in fostering a culture of entrepreneurship in the community. Through his informal networks and relationships, he connects budding entrepreneurs with resources and mentorship opportunities. These efforts contribute to a growing ecosystem of local businesses, which begin to transform the economic landscape of the community.

Another significant aspect of Thabo's unseen influence is his involvement in local environmental initiatives. Recognizing the importance of sustainable development, Thabo quietly supports projects that promote environmental stewardship. From community recycling programs to urban gardening projects, his subtle guidance helps inculcate a sense of responsibility towards the environment.

The narrative then shifts to a personal reflection by Thabo. He contemplates the changes he has witnessed and influenced in his community. This reflection is a mix of pride and humility – pride in seeing the positive changes and humility in understanding that these changes are the result of collective effort, not just his own.

Thabo's influence also extends to the arts and culture of the community. He supports local artists and cultural groups, often anonymously, helping to preserve and promote the community's rich cultural heritage. These cultural activities strengthen community bonds and provide a source of joy and pride for the residents.

A poignant moment in the chapter occurs when Thabo visits the tech incubator he once spearheaded. Now run by a group of young entrepreneurs he mentored; the incubator has become a dynamic hub of innovation. Thabo's quiet pride in their achievements reflects the fulfilment he finds in seeing others succeed.

As "Unseen Influence" concludes, the community organizes a celebration to honour its unsung heroes – individuals who have contributed significantly to the community's growth without seeking recognition. Thabo is one of those honoured, though he insists that the real heroes are the members of the community who continue to work tirelessly for its betterment.

The chapter ends with Thabo at the celebration, watching the community come together in a vibrant display of unity and strength. "Unseen Influence" closes with a message of hope and a reminder that leadership can take many forms, often the most impactful being those that quietly nurture and empower others. Thabo's journey becomes a powerful illustration of how one person's commitment to service can ignite a chain reaction of positive change, leaving a lasting legacy in the community.

THE LEGACY CONTINUES

The Legacy Continues, Thabo Mokoena's journey reaches a stage where his impact is deeply embedded in the fabric of his community, transcending his direct involvement. This chapter is a celebration of the enduring legacy of Thabo's work and the continued growth and development of his community.

The chapter opens with a reflective Thabo observing the positive changes in his community. Over the years, the initiatives he started or influenced have grown and evolved, taking on lives of their own. He sees a community that is more empowered, vibrant, and resilient, a testament to the collective efforts and shared vision of its members.

A key theme of "The Legacy Continues" is the sustainability of Thabo's initiatives. The community centre, now a cornerstone of the community, runs various programs addressing education, health, entrepreneurship, and cultural activities. The leadership of these programs has been passed on to capable community members who share Thabo's passion and commitment.

The tech incubator has become a beacon of innovation and entrepreneurship, attracting young talents from across the region. It stands as a symbol of the community's progress and its ability to adapt to the changing economic landscape.

The success stories emerging from the incubator inspire the next generation of entrepreneurs. The soccer team, which Thabo had nurtured, continues to be a source of pride and unity. It has established itself as a formidable force in regional leagues and is involved in various community outreach programs. The team's success on and off the field is a reflection of the values and principles instilled by Thabo.

Thabo's influence extends beyond specific projects. He has inspired a culture of service and leadership in the community. There are stories of individuals and groups who, motivated by Thabo's example, have initiated their projects and advocacy efforts, addressing various community needs and challenges.

The narrative then shifts to a community event celebrating the achievements of the past years. At this event, Thabo is honoured for his contributions, but he redirects the accolades to the community, emphasizing the collective effort behind their success. This event is not just a celebration of achievements but also a reaffirmation of the community's commitment to continue working towards a better future.

As "The Legacy Continues" concludes, Thabo takes a moment to reflect on his journey. He feels a sense of fulfilment, knowing that his efforts have contributed to building a strong, self-reliant community. He understands that his legacy is not about individual accolades but about the empowerment and success of the community as a whole.

The chapter ends with Thabo looking forward to the future, content in the knowledge that the seeds he has planted will continue to grow and flourish in the hands of the community. "The Legacy Continues" is a testament to the enduring impact of visionary leadership and the power of community-driven change. It closes with a sense of hope and optimism, as the legacy of Thabo Mokoena lives on in the vibrant, thriving community he helped to shape.

As "The Legacy Continues" progresses, the enduring impact of Thabo Mokoena's life's work becomes increasingly evident, painting a picture of a community that has not only embraced his vision but also expanded upon it.

The chapter delves into various success stories within the community, each a reflection of Thabo's influence. A young woman, inspired by Thabo's mentorship, launches a successful social enterprise focused on sustainable farming, providing employment opportunities and promoting environmental stewardship. Another group of youth, once participants in the leadership program at the community centre, now lead a local initiative promoting digital literacy among the elderly, bridging the generational divide.

Thabo's role in the community has evolved. He is no longer the driving force but rather a revered figure whose advice and wisdom are sought after.

He engages with the community in a more consultative capacity, offering guidance when needed but largely allowing the new generation of leaders to chart their course. The narrative then focuses on a special project that holds personal significance for Thabo – a history and cultural preservation initiative. This project, which he helped to conceive, aims to document and celebrate the community's history, including its struggles and triumphs. It serves as a reminder of the community's journey and a source of inspiration for future generations.

A moving aspect of the chapter is when Thabo revisits the soccer field, where it all began. He watches a match, seeing the vibrant energy and camaraderie of the players. The field is no longer just a sporting ground; it has become a community landmark, embodying the spirit of unity and perseverance that Thabo always championed.

As "The Legacy Continues" nears its conclusion, the community organizes a tribute event for Thabo. It's an emotional gathering, attended by individuals whose lives have been touched by Thabo's work. The event features stories, performances, and testimonials celebrating Thabo's impact. While Thabo is humbled by the recognition, he reiterates that the community's achievements are the result of collective effort and shared vision.

The chapter closes with Thabo delivering a speech at the event. He reflects on the journey, expressing his gratitude and hope for the future.

He talks about the power of community, the importance of resilience, and the belief that change is possible when people come together for a common cause.

"The Legacy Continues" concludes with a sense of fulfilment and completion. Thabo's legacy is not just in the projects he started or the direct changes he implemented but in the spirit of empowerment, unity, and progress that he instilled in the community. The chapter ends with a panoramic view of the thriving community, a living testament to Thabo Mokoena's life and work, and a symbol of hope and resilience that will continue to inspire generations to come.

SECRETS OF SUCCESS

In "Secrets of Success," Thabo Mokoena shares the wisdom and insights gained through his extensive journey of community leadership and development. This chapter is a rich tapestry of experiences and lessons that Thabo has accumulated over the years, distilled into key principles that have underpinned his successful endeavours.

Thabo begins by emphasizing the importance of having a clear, guiding vision. He reflects on how his vision for a transformed, empowered community served as a beacon through various challenges. Persistence, he notes, is equally crucial; it's the driving force that kept him moving forward, even in the face of adversity.

A significant aspect of Thabo's approach is community engagement. He believes that lasting change is rooted in the community. Understanding and involving the community in every aspect of the development process is essential for the success of any initiative. This engagement fosters a sense of ownership and ensures that efforts are tailored to meet the community's actual needs.

Adaptability is another critical factor that Thabo highlights. He shares his experiences of navigating a constantly changing landscape, emphasizing the need to be flexible and responsive. Adapting strategies in response to new challenges, information, and opportunities is vital for maintaining relevance and effectiveness.

Thabo also talks about the power of empowerment and mentorship. By empowering others to lead and providing support and guidance, he has been able to create a sustainable impact that goes beyond his direct involvement. This approach has enabled the emergence of new leaders within the community, ensuring the continuity and growth of initiatives.

Integrity and transparency are foundational elements of Thabo's philosophy. He discusses the importance of maintaining ethical standards and being transparent in actions and decisions. This approach has helped him build trust and credibility, which are crucial in community work.

Collaborative partnerships have been instrumental in amplifying Thabo's impact. He underscores the value of working with various stakeholders, including government entities, private sector players, and other community organizations. These collaborations have enabled him to scale the reach and effectiveness of his initiatives, creating more significant change.

Finally, Thabo speaks about the importance of resilience. He shares personal anecdotes of overcoming difficulties, emphasizing that resilience is key to navigating the often-turbulent journey of social change. Challenges, he believes, should be seen as opportunities for growth and learning.

As the chapter concludes, Thabo's message of perseverance, community engagement, adaptability, empowerment, integrity, collaborative partnerships, and resilience resonates deeply with the audience. His interaction with individuals after the forum, offering personal advice and encouragement, symbolizes his ongoing commitment to nurturing and guiding future leaders.

"Secrets of Success" is more than a reflection on Thabo's journey; it is a valuable guide for effective leadership and meaningful social change, offering insights and inspiration for anyone committed to making a positive impact in their community or field.

As "Secrets of Success" continues, Thabo Mokoena delves deeper into the nuances of what has made his and his community's journey impactful and transformative. He shares more insights, drawing from a well of experiences, each underlining the multifaceted nature of successful community leadership and development.

Thabo talks about the significance of learning from both successes and failures. He emphasizes that each setback and triumph has been a learning opportunity, shaping his approach and strategies. He encourages emerging leaders to embrace their mistakes as crucial steps in their growth process, highlighting that resilience is not just about enduring challenges, but also about learning from them and evolving.

Another key aspect Thabo touches upon is the importance of self-care in leadership. He shares how, in his journey, there were moments of burnout and how he learned the hard way that one cannot pour from an empty cup. He stresses the need for leaders to take care of their physical and mental well-being, as it is essential for sustaining their ability to serve effectively.

Thabo also reflects on the importance of community culture and identity. He talks about the efforts made to nurture a sense of community pride and belonging, fostering an environment where people feel valued and connected. He points out that strong community bonds are the bedrock upon which sustainable development can be built.

In discussing the evolution of his role over time, Thabo notes the shift from being a direct leader to a mentor and advisor. He elaborates on the importance of this transition, explaining how it allowed for the emergence of new ideas and leadership styles within the community, which were crucial for its dynamic growth and adaptability.

Thabo also highlights the role of patience in effecting social change. He acknowledges that change is often a slow process and that it requires persistence and the willingness to stay the course, even when results are not immediately visible.

Towards the end of the chapter, Thabo addresses the future generations. He underscores the importance of passing down the values of service, community engagement, and ethical leadership. He envisions a future where the seeds he has planted continue to grow and flourish, nurtured by the hands of those who come after him.

"Secrets of Success" concludes with Thabo at a community gathering, surrounded by people whose lives have been touched by his work. As he listens to their stories and shares in their celebrations, Thabo feels a profound sense of fulfilment.

The chapter closes with a reaffirmation of his belief in the power of community, the transformative nature of collaborative effort, and the enduring impact of leading with integrity, compassion, and resilience. "Secrets of Success" is not just the story of Thabo Mokoena's journey; it is a testament to the collective journey of a community that rose to realize its potential through shared struggles, dreams, and triumphs.

EMPOWERING THE NEXT GENERATION

Empowering the Next Generation, Thabo Mokoena focuses on nurturing and guiding the future leaders of his community. This chapter is a narrative about passing the torch, as Thabo invests his energy and wisdom into ensuring that the next generation is equipped to continue the work of building a thriving, resilient community.

The chapter opens with Thabo reflecting on the importance of investing in youth. He recognizes that the longevity and sustainability of the community's progress depend on the active involvement and leadership of younger generations. To this end, Thabo dedicates himself to developing programs and initiatives aimed at empowering young people.

A key focus of Thabo's efforts is education. He works closely with local schools and educational institutions to enhance the quality of education and to ensure that it is accessible to all. He advocates for curriculums that not only provide academic knowledge but also teach critical thinking, civic responsibility, and leadership skills.

Thabo also establishes a youth mentorship program, were experienced community leaders' mentor young individuals. This program provides a platform for intergenerational dialogue and learning, where the wisdom of experience meets the innovation and energy of youth.

In addition to mentorship, Thabo fosters entrepreneurial skills among the youth. He expands the tech incubator to include a youth entrepreneurship program, providing training, resources, and support to young aspiring entrepreneurs. This initiative helps cultivate a culture of innovation and self-reliance among the younger members of the community.

Another significant aspect of Thabo's work is encouraging civic engagement among the youth. He organizes workshops and forums where young people can learn about and discuss community issues, governance, and social change. Thabo believes in the importance of having an informed, engaged youth population that actively participates in shaping the community's future.

The narrative then shifts to highlight the impact of these initiatives. Stories emerge of young individuals who, inspired and supported by Thabo's programs, start their projects, lead community development efforts, or take on leadership roles within existing initiatives. These young leaders become a testament to the success of Thabo's efforts to empower the next generation.

As "Empowering the Next Generation" draws to a close, Thabo attends a community event where young leaders showcase their projects and share their visions for the future. Thabo listens with pride and hope, seeing in these young faces the future of the community he has dedicated his life to serving.

Thabo reflecting on the cycle of mentorship and leadership. He realizes that his greatest legacy is not the projects he started or the changes he implemented, but the spark of potential he has ignited in the next generation. "Empowering the Next Generation" closes with a sense of continuity and renewal, as Thabo's journey merges into the paths of those he has inspired and mentored, ensuring that the community's progress continues into the future.

As "Empowering the Next Generation" continues, Thabo Mokoena's commitment to fostering the growth and development of young leaders in his community becomes increasingly impactful, shaping the future trajectory of the community's progress.

The narrative explores the expanding influence of the youth mentorship program. Thabo ensures that this program is not just about providing guidance but also about giving young individuals the space to lead and innovate. He encourages them to take on significant roles in community projects, providing them with real-world experience and responsibility.

Thabo also places a strong emphasis on cultural and social awareness. He organizes events and workshops that delve into the community's history, culture, and social issues.
These sessions are designed to instil a sense of identity and belonging in the youth, as well as an understanding of their role in shaping the community's cultural and social landscape.

A significant development in the chapter is the establishment of a youth council, a platform where young people can voice their ideas and concerns, and actively participate in community decision-making processes. Thabo mentors the council members, guiding them in effective leadership and governance, while ensuring that they have the autonomy to make their own decisions.

Thabo's efforts in promoting education extend beyond the classroom. He advocates for experiential learning opportunities, such as internships and community service projects, that complement formal education. These experiences are crucial in developing practical skills and a deeper understanding of social dynamics and community development.

The impact of Thabo's initiatives begins to show as young leaders start to emerge from various programs. These young leaders take on active roles in addressing community issues, from environmental projects to social welfare initiatives. They bring fresh perspectives and innovative approaches, signalling a vibrant future for the community.

As the chapter nears its conclusion, Thabo reflects on the journey of empowering the next generation. He attends a community celebration where young leaders present their achievements and future plans. Thabo feels a sense of accomplishment, seeing the seeds he has sown bear fruit in the form of capable, confident young individuals ready to lead their community into the future.

"Empowering the Next Generation" concludes with Thabo addressing the gathering, sharing his hopes and aspirations for these young leaders. He emphasizes the importance of continuous learning, community service, and ethical leadership. The chapter closes with a sense of hope and continuity, as Thabo's legacy is secured in the hands of the empowered and inspired youth, ready to carry forward the torch of community development and social change.

SOCCER TEAM'S INTERNATIONAL GLORY

Soccer Team's International Glory, the narrative takes a celebratory turn, focusing on the remarkable achievements of the soccer team that Thabo Mokoena nurtured from its humble beginnings. The chapter highlights the team's ascent to international recognition, symbolizing the global impact of community-driven initiatives.

The chapter opens with the soccer team, which has become a cornerstone of the community under Thabo's mentorship, preparing for an international tournament. This opportunity marks a significant milestone, not only for the team but also for the community, showcasing their talent and unity on a global stage.

Thabo, while no longer directly managing the team, remains a key figure in their journey. His foundational work in establishing the team and instilling values of hard work, teamwork, and community pride has paved the way for this moment. The team's participation in the international tournament is as much a tribute to Thabo's vision as it is a testament to the players' dedication and skill.

The narrative then delves into the preparations for the tournament. The community rallies around the team, offering support in various forms – from fundraising efforts to morale-boosting events. The excitement and unity within the community are palpable, with everyone feeling a part of the team's journey.

As the tournament begins, the soccer team faces tough competition from well-established teams from around the world. However, their unique style of play, honed in the local fields of their community, sets them apart. The team's performance is not just about showcasing their football skills; it's a display of their community's spirit and resilience.

A highlight of the chapter is a dramatic match where the team secures a significant victory against a top-ranked opponent. This victory sends ripples of excitement and pride throughout the community and the nation. The team's success becomes a source of national pride, putting not just the team but their community and Thabo's work on the international map.

Thabo watches the tournament from home, filled with pride and emotion. He sees in the team's success the realization of a dream that began many years ago on a makeshift soccer field in the community. The team's international glory is a culmination of years of hard work, dedication, and belief in the potential of the community's youth.

As the chapter concludes, the team returns home to a hero's welcome. The community's celebration is a vibrant affair, filled with joy and a sense of collective accomplishment. Thabo joins the celebration, not as the team's founder but as a proud member of the community.

"Soccer Team's International Glory" closes with a reflective Thabo acknowledging the far-reaching impact of the team's success. The chapter is a celebration of how local initiatives can achieve global recognition and how community-driven projects can transcend boundaries and inspire people worldwide. It is a testament to the power of sports as a unifying force and a source of community pride and international acclaim.

As "Soccer Team's International Glory" progresses, the story delves deeper into the aftermath of the team's remarkable achievement and its broader implications for the community and beyond.

In the wake of the tournament, the soccer team becomes a symbol of hope and inspiration not only for their community but also for similar communities across the nation and internationally. Their success story resonates widely, highlighting the potential of grassroots sports initiatives to achieve greatness against all odds.

Thabo, while watching these developments, feels a deep sense of fulfilment. He had always believed in the power of sports to unite and uplift, and the team's international success is a vivid realization of this belief. The team's victory goes beyond the realm of sports; it becomes a narrative of overcoming limitations and redefining possibilities.

The narrative then explores how the soccer team's success brings newfound attention and resources to the community. Invitations for friendly matches and tournaments start pouring in from different parts of the world, offering the team further opportunities to showcase their talent. The team's exposure to different playing styles and cultures becomes a valuable learning experience, enhancing their skills and broadening their perspectives.

Thabo seizes this opportunity to further develop the community's sports programs. Inspired by the team's success, he initiates more sports-related community development projects. These include establishing sports academies for the youth, improving sports facilities, and creating exchange programs with teams in other countries.

The soccer team's glory also revitalizes the community's economy. The influx of visitors and the increased media attention led to new business opportunities, boosting local enterprises and tourism. The community begins to be recognized as a hub of sporting excellence, attracting investment and partnerships.

As the chapter nears its conclusion, Thabo organizes a community event to celebrate the team's achievements and to discuss the future of sports in the community. The event is a gathering of community members, local leaders, and representatives from sports organizations. It's a forum for discussing how sports can continue to be a vehicle for positive change and development.

"Soccer Team's International Glory" concludes with Thabo addressing the gathering, reflecting on the journey of the soccer team and its wider impact. He talks about the unifying power of sports, the importance of nurturing young talent, and the role of community support in achieving success.

The chapter closes with a sense of collective pride and hope for the future. Thabo's legacy, embodied in the soccer team's international success, is a source of inspiration, not just for aspiring athletes, but for anyone striving to make a positive impact in their community. The soccer team's story is a testament to the extraordinary possibilities that can arise from humble beginnings and the enduring impact of community-driven initiatives.

A COMMUNITY TRANSFORMED

A Community Transformed, the narrative chronicles the profound changes that have taken place in Thabo Mokoena's community, painting a picture of transformation driven by collective effort and visionary leadership. This chapter is a reflection on how far the community has come and the factors that have contributed to its metamorphosis.

The chapter opens with a panoramic view of the community, now bustling with activity and vibrancy. The changes are evident in the improved infrastructure, the thriving local businesses, and the vibrant cultural and recreational spaces. The community, once struggling with various socio-economic challenges, has become a model of sustainable development and social cohesion.

Thabo, walking through the community, takes in the changes with a sense of quiet satisfaction. He reflects on the journey that brought them here - the initial struggles, the setbacks, the victories, and the unwavering spirit of the community members. It's a journey marked by collective determination and resilience.

One of the key aspects of the community's transformation is the quality of education. The local schools, with the support of Thabo's initiatives, have become centres of excellence, providing high-quality education and fostering a culture of learning and curiosity.

These schools are now producing graduates who are well-equipped to pursue higher education and meaningful careers. The narrative then shifts to the economic transformation of the community. The local economy has diversified, with the growth of small and medium enterprises and the establishment of cooperative businesses.

These economic changes have led to job creation and increased economic stability for many families. The community's entrepreneurs, many of whom were mentored in Thabo's programs, are now key drivers of this economic vibrancy.

Health and wellness have also become a focus in the community. The health initiatives started by Thabo have evolved, leading to better healthcare facilities, increased health awareness, and improved overall community health. These initiatives have been crucial in addressing long-standing health challenges and promoting a culture of wellness.

Thabo's influence is also evident in the community's social fabric. The various cultural and sports programs have not only provided recreational outlets but have also fostered a strong sense of community identity and pride. The soccer team's success, in particular, has become a source of communal pride, uniting people across different backgrounds.

As "A Community Transformed" draws to a close, Thabo participates in a community celebration event. The event is a reflection of the community's journey, featuring cultural performances, exhibitions from local businesses, and testimonials from community members. Thabo is honoured at the event, but he redirects the accolades to the community, emphasizing the collective nature of their achievements.

The chapter ends with Thabo delivering a speech at the event, where he reflects on the power of community, the importance of shared vision and hard work, and the endless possibilities that arise when people come together for a common cause. "A Community Transformed" closes with a sense of accomplishment and optimism, as the community, inspired by Thabo's vision and dedication, continues to thrive and evolve, setting an example for others to follow.

As "A Community Transformed" progresses, the story delves deeper into the various facets of the community's transformation, highlighting the lasting impact of the initiatives and the new challenges and opportunities that have emerged.

The narrative explores the evolution of the community's environmental consciousness. Under Thabo's guidance, sustainable practices have been integrated into various aspects of community life.
There are now green spaces, community gardens, and recycling programs that not only enhance the environment but also foster a sense of collective responsibility and stewardship among the residents.

Thabo takes a moment to visit the tech incubator, which has become a symbol of innovation and progress in the community. The incubator, now self-sustaining, is a launchpad for numerous successful start-ups, contributing significantly to the local economy. It's a hub where young, creative minds come together to solve problems and develop new technologies.

The chapter then highlights the community's cultural renaissance. Art and cultural festivals have become regular events, celebrating the diverse heritage and talent within the community. These events draw visitors from outside the community, enhancing cultural exchange and understanding. Thabo's support for these initiatives underscores his belief in the power of culture to unite and inspire.

An important development in the chapter is the community's increasing involvement in regional and national issues. The success of the community has not gone unnoticed, and its leaders, many of whom were mentored by Thabo, are now influencing policy and decision-making at higher levels. This influence is a testament to the community's growing prominence and the effectiveness of its grassroots leadership model.

As the chapter nears its conclusion, Thabo reflects on the changing dynamics within the community. He sees a new generation of leaders emerging, ready to take on the mantle and bring fresh perspectives and ideas. This transition is bittersweet for Thabo, but he recognizes it as a necessary and positive step towards the community's ongoing evolution.

"A Community Transformed" concludes with a community assembly where Thabo is asked to share his thoughts on the future. He speaks about the importance of continual growth and adaptation, the need to remain united in the face of new challenges, and the enduring power of community spirit. His words are met with applause and nods of agreement, a sign of the deep respect and admiration the community holds for him.

With Thabo looking out over the assembled crowd, a tapestry of faces young and old, all united by a shared journey. It's a moment of profound fulfilment for Thabo, seeing the community he has nurtured stand strong, vibrant, and forward-looking. "A Community Transformed" is a tribute to the power of community-driven change, the resilience of the human spirit, and the enduring impact of visionary leadership.

As "A Community Transformed" progresses, the story delves deeper into the various facets of the community's transformation, highlighting the lasting impact of the initiatives and the new challenges and opportunities that have emerged.

The narrative explores the evolution of the community's environmental consciousness. Under Thabo's guidance, sustainable practices have been integrated into various aspects of community life. There are now green spaces, community gardens, and recycling programs that not only enhance the environment but also foster a sense of collective responsibility and stewardship among the residents.

Thabo takes a moment to visit the tech incubator, which has become a symbol of innovation and progress in the community. The incubator, now self-sustaining, is a launchpad for numerous successful start-ups, contributing significantly to the local economy. It's a hub where young, creative minds come together to solve problems and develop new technologies.

The chapter then highlights the community's cultural renaissance. Art and cultural festivals have become regular events, celebrating the diverse heritage and talent within the community. These events draw visitors from outside the community, enhancing cultural exchange and understanding. Thabo's support for these initiatives underscores his belief in the power of culture to unite and inspire.

An important development in the chapter is the community's increasing involvement in regional and national issues. The success of the community has not gone unnoticed, and its leaders, many of whom were mentored by Thabo, are now influencing policy and decision-making at higher levels. This influence is a testament to the community's growing prominence and the effectiveness of its grassroots leadership model.

As the chapter nears its conclusion, Thabo reflects on the changing dynamics within the community. He sees a new generation of leaders emerging, ready to take on the mantle and bring fresh perspectives and ideas. This transition is bittersweet for Thabo, but he recognizes it as a necessary and positive step towards the community's ongoing evolution.

"A Community Transformed" concludes with a community assembly where Thabo is asked to share his thoughts on the future. He speaks about the importance of continual growth and adaptation, the need to remain united in the face of new challenges, and the enduring power of community spirit. His words are met with applause and nods of agreement, a sign of the deep respect and admiration the community holds for him.

The chapter closes with Thabo looking out over the assembled crowd, a tapestry of faces young and old, all united by a shared journey. It's a moment of profound fulfilment for Thabo, seeing the community he has nurtured stand strong, vibrant, and forward-looking. "A Community Transformed" is a tribute to the power of community-driven change, the resilience of the human spirit, and the enduring impact of visionary leadership.

REVELATION OF THE PAST

Revelation of the Past, the narrative takes a reflective turn as Thabo Mokoena confronts and reconciles with aspects of his past that have shaped his journey and the community's evolution. This chapter delves into the hidden stories and experiences that have influenced Thabo, offering a deeper understanding of his motivations and resilience.

The chapter begins with Thabo discovering a collection of old letters and photographs in his attic, artifacts from his early life and the initial years of his community work. As he sifts through these mementos, memories resurface, some long-forgotten, revealing layers of his past that have quietly influenced his path.

Among the letters, Thabo finds correspondences with old mentors and friends, some of whom had played pivotal roles in his early development as a leader. These letters bring back stories of struggle, support, and inspiration, highlighting the collective effort behind his achievements. Thabo is reminded of the importance of the support and guidance he received, shaping his philosophy of mentorship and community involvement.

Thabo then comes across photographs of the community in its earlier days, starkly contrasting with its current state. These images serve as a poignant reminder of the journey they have all undertaken.

They depict the challenges they faced – poverty, social unrest, and a lack of resources – and the communal spirit that helped them overcome these obstacles.

A significant moment in the chapter occurs when Thabo discovers a series of journals he had kept during the community's most challenging times. The journals reveal his inner thoughts and doubts, his fears and hopes during those formative years. Reading through them, Thabo reconnects with the motivations that drove him and the lessons learned along the way.

The narrative then explores how this journey into the past impacts Thabo's present. He shares these discoveries with the community, organizing an exhibition that includes the photographs, letters, and excerpts from his journals. This exhibition becomes a powerful tool for community reflection and bonding, as members young and old gather to share stories and learn about their collective history.

As "Revelation of the Past" draws to a close, Thabo leads a community discussion at the exhibition. He talks openly about his journey, the challenges he faced, and the invaluable support he received. He emphasizes the importance of remembering and learning from the past while looking forward to the future.

The chapter concludes with Thabo feeling a renewed sense of connection with his community and his own journey. "Revelation of the Past" is a testament to the power of history and memory in shaping our paths and our communities. It closes with a community more united and aware of its shared history and the individual journeys that have woven together to create its present.

As "Revelation of the Past" progresses, Thabo Mokoena's journey through his own history and the community's shared experiences deepens, shedding light on the pivotal moments and decisions that have shaped their collective destiny.

The exhibition of Thabo's old letters, photographs, and journals becomes a focal point for the community, sparking conversations about their shared history and heritage. Elder members of the community, inspired by Thabo's revelations, begin to share their own stories and memories, weaving a rich tapestry of the community's journey. These narratives highlight the struggles, triumphs, and unyielding spirit of the community over the years.

A profound moment in the chapter occurs when Thabo discovers a series of articles and news clippings about the community's early activism. These clippings reveal the community's role in broader social and political movements, highlighting its contributions to larger causes. This discovery brings a sense of pride and also a deeper understanding of the community's place in the wider historical context.

Thabo then finds a series of personal notes and reflections he wrote during critical turning points in the community's development. These writings provide insight into Thabo's mindset during those times – his doubts, his decision-making processes, and his hopes for the community's future. Sharing these reflections with the community, Thabo opens up about the challenges of leadership and the importance of staying true to one's values and vision.

The narrative also explores how this exploration of the past influences the younger generation. The youth, inspired by the stories and histories uncovered, begin to see their community in a new light. They gain a greater appreciation for the sacrifices and efforts of the generations before them, fostering a sense of responsibility to continue the legacy.

As "Revelation of the Past" nears its end, Thabo organizes a community storytelling event. This event becomes a celebration of the community's history, with people of all ages sharing stories, experiences, and lessons learned. It's a moment of collective reflection, recognition, and bonding, strengthening the community's sense of identity and purpose.

The chapter concludes with Thabo reflecting on the power of understanding and embracing the past. He realizes that acknowledging and learning from the past is crucial in shaping a more conscious and resilient community.

"Revelation of the Past" closes with a community that is more connected to its history, more aware of its strengths and challenges, and more united in its journey towards a shared future. It's a powerful reminder of how revisiting and embracing our history can illuminate our present and guide our path forward.

FACING OLD DEMONS

Facing Old Demons, Thabo Mokoena confronts unresolved challenges and personal battles from his past. This chapter delves into the internal struggles and external conflicts that Thabo has had to navigate, shedding light on the resilience and growth that often come from facing one's demons.

The chapter begins with Thabo receiving news of a resurgence of an old conflict within the community, a reminder of the struggles he thought were long overcome. This conflict, stemming from deep-seated issues in the community's past, forces Thabo to revisit and address some of the unresolved tensions that have been simmering beneath the surface.

As Thabo grapples with this renewed challenge, he is also confronted with personal demons from his past. A figure from Thabo's early days in the community, a former adversary, re-emerges, bringing back memories of past conflicts and the difficult decisions Thabo had to make. This encounter forces Thabo to reflect on his journey, the choices he has made, and the impact they have had on his life and the community.

The narrative then shifts to Thabo's efforts to resolve the rekindled conflict in the community. He engages with different groups, facilitating dialogues and negotiations.

These discussions are tense and emotional, as they bring to light long-standing grievances and misunderstandings. Thabo's approach is one of empathy and honesty, as he seeks to foster understanding and reconciliation.

In dealing with his personal demons, Thabo embarks on a journey of introspection. He revisits old diaries and journals, reflecting on his growth and the lessons learned over the years. This process is challenging but cathartic, as Thabo confronts and comes to terms with his past actions and their consequences.

A poignant moment in the chapter occurs when Thabo has a heart-to-heart conversation with his former adversary. This conversation is a turning point, as both individuals express their perspectives and grievances. The dialogue leads to a mutual understanding and, eventually, a sense of closure and forgiveness.

As "Facing Old Demons" draws to a close, Thabo manages to mediate a resolution to the community conflict. The resolution is not just a settlement of the immediate issues but a step towards healing deeper wounds within the community. Thabo's role in navigating this complex situation reinforces his position as a respected and wise leader.

Thabo feeling a sense of peace and resolution, both personally and for the community. "Facing Old Demons" is a testament to the importance of confronting and resolving past conflicts for personal growth and community harmony. It closes with a reinforced sense of hope and unity in the community, as they move forward stronger and more cohesive, having faced and overcome their demons together.

As "Facing Old Demons" continues, Thabo Mokoena's personal journey of introspection and the community's process of healing and reconciliation deepen, offering a profound look at the complexities of overcoming historical conflicts and personal struggles.

Thabo's confrontation with his past leads him to realize the importance of acknowledging and addressing the root causes of longstanding issues. He initiates a series of community workshops focused on healing and understanding. These workshops provide a safe space for members of the community to share their experiences, voice their concerns, and work together towards resolving deep-seated issues.

In parallel to addressing community conflicts, Thabo faces his own internal battles. He reflects on his life's journey, acknowledging the mistakes he made and the lessons he learned. This process of self-reflection is difficult but necessary for Thabo's personal growth. He comes to terms with the fact that his actions, while well-intentioned, may have had unintended consequences, and he learns to forgive himself and move forward.

A significant development in the chapter is Thabo's effort to strengthen community cohesion. Recognizing that the resilience of the community lies in its unity, he focuses on building bridges between different groups within the community. He organizes joint projects and events that encourage collaboration and mutual understanding, helping to mend rifts and foster a sense of shared purpose.

The narrative then explores how the younger generation in the community responds to these efforts. Inspired by Thabo's example and the ongoing reconciliation processes, they take an active role in promoting peace and unity. Young leaders emerge, taking the initiative to organize events and projects that celebrate the community's diversity and promote inclusiveness.

As the chapter nears its conclusion, Thabo is invited to speak at a local gathering. He shares his reflections on the importance of facing and overcoming past demons, both personally and as a community. He talks about the power of forgiveness, the strength found in unity, and the need for continuous dialogue and empathy to resolve conflicts.

"Facing Old Demons" concludes with a renewed sense of hope and resilience in the community. The process of confronting and working through past issues has brought the community closer, making it stronger and more united. Thabo, having faced his own demons, feels a sense of liberation and clarity, ready to continue his work with a deeper understanding and renewed purpose.

The chapter closes with the community moving forward, not by forgetting the past, but by learning from it and using those lessons to build a stronger, more harmonious future. "Facing Old Demons" is a powerful reminder of the healing that comes from facing our challenges head-on and the transformative impact this process can have on individuals and communities alike.

TRUTH AND RECONCILIATION

Truth and Reconciliation, the narrative explores the community's journey towards healing and unity, with Thabo Mokoena playing a crucial role in facilitating this process. This chapter delves into the complex dynamics of addressing historical grievances and fostering a sense of collective healing and understanding.

The chapter begins with the community grappling with its past. Long-standing issues, stemming from historical injustices and conflicts, have left deep scars. Thabo recognizes the need for a structured process to address these issues, inspired by the national Truth and Reconciliation Commission. He proposes a community-level truth and reconciliation forum, aiming to provide a platform for open dialogue, healing, and restoration.

Thabo's proposal is met with mixed reactions. While some members of the community embrace the idea, others are sceptical, fearing that reopening old wounds might lead to more division. Thabo navigates these concerns with empathy and determination, emphasizing the importance of confronting the past to build a more united and peaceful future.

The narrative then shifts to the organization of the forum. Thabo, along with a team of community leaders and facilitators, sets up a series of meetings and workshops.

These sessions are designed to allow community members to share their experiences and grievances in a safe and respectful environment. The process is emotional and challenging, as painful memories and stories come to the fore.

A poignant moment in the chapter occurs when individuals from opposing sides of past conflicts come forward to share their stories. These testimonies are powerful and heart-breaking, revealing the depth of pain and misunderstanding that has existed within the community. However, they also open the door to empathy and understanding.

As the forum progresses, Thabo and the facilitators guide the community through a process of acknowledgment and forgiveness. They introduce activities and discussions focused on healing and reconciliation, encouraging participants to see each other's perspectives and to find common ground.

The narrative also explores how the younger generation participates in and is impacted by the forum. Young people, who may not have directly experienced the past conflicts, gain a deeper understanding of their community's history. They play a key role in the reconciliation process, bridging generational divides and bringing new energy to the pursuit of unity and peace.

As "Truth and Reconciliation" draws to a close, the community begins to experience a sense of closure and renewal. The forum has not solved all the issues, but it has set the community on a path of healing and mutual understanding. The process has strengthened the community's social fabric, creating a more cohesive and empathetic environment.

With a community gathering, where reflections on the forum and its outcomes are shared. Thabo speaks at the gathering, emphasizing the ongoing nature of the reconciliation process and the importance of continuing to work together for a harmonious community.

"Truth and Reconciliation" closes with a sense of hope and a renewed commitment to building a community grounded in understanding, respect, and unity. It's a testament to the power of facing the truth, the healing that comes with reconciliation, and the strength of a community that chooses to move forward together.

As "Truth and Reconciliation" unfolds, the community's journey through the difficult yet essential process of healing and coming to terms with its past continues, under the empathetic guidance of Thabo Mokoena.

Following the initial forums, Thabo realizes the need for ongoing efforts to maintain the momentum of reconciliation. He helps establish a permanent community committee dedicated to truth and reconciliation.

This committee, comprising members from different backgrounds and experiences within the community, works to ensure that the dialogue continues and that the lessons learned are integrated into the community's daily life.

Thabo also focuses on educational initiatives to instil the values of understanding and empathy in the younger generation. In collaboration with local schools, he helps develop curricula that include the community's history, the principles of reconciliation, and the importance of diversity and inclusivity. These educational efforts aim to prevent the repetition of past mistakes and to foster a culture of peace and mutual respect among the community's youth.

The narrative then explores the impact of these initiatives on the community. Gradually, there's a noticeable shift in interactions and relationships. People who were once divided start working together on community projects, bridging gaps that had existed for years. The atmosphere in the community becomes more open and inclusive, with increased participation in communal activities and decision-making.

An emotionally powerful moment in the chapter occurs when a commemoration event is organized. This event honours both the struggles and the progress of the community. It includes testimonies from those who have suffered, acknowledgments of past wrongs, and commitments to a shared future. The event is cathartic, solidifying the community's resolve to move forward in unity.

As "Truth and Reconciliation" progresses, Thabo's role as a facilitator and mentor becomes increasingly crucial. He is seen as a stabilizing force, someone who has not only lived through the community's darkest times but who has also been instrumental in guiding it towards a brighter future. His wisdom and balanced approach continue to inspire and guide the community.

Towards the end of the chapter, Thabo reflects on the transformation he has witnessed. He feels a profound sense of accomplishment, not just in terms of the tangible changes in the community but also in the shift in mindset and attitude among its members. He recognizes that while the journey of reconciliation is never truly complete, the community has laid a strong foundation for continued healing and growth.

"Truth and Reconciliation" concludes with a sense of cautious optimism. The community, having confronted its past and embarked on a path of healing, looks forward to a future where diversity is celebrated, and unity is strengthened. The chapter closes with a reminder of the power of honest dialogue, empathy, and the enduring human capacity for forgiveness and renewal.

MENDING BROKEN BRIDGES

Mending Broken Bridges, the narrative shifts to focus on Thabo Mokoena's efforts to repair relationships and rebuild connections within the community that had been strained or broken due to past conflicts and misunderstandings. This chapter delves into the challenges and triumphs of restoring unity and harmony in a community working towards a common future.

The chapter opens with Thabo addressing a delicate situation within the community. A long-standing dispute between two prominent local families, which had caused a rift in the community, comes to the forefront. Thabo, with his deep understanding of the community's dynamics and history, steps in to mediate the situation.

Thabo's approach is one of patience and impartiality. He meets with each family separately, listening to their grievances and perspectives. He helps them to see the broader impact of their feud on the community and encourages them to consider the benefits of reconciliation. Thabo's mediation is challenging, as years of mistrust and resentment have built up, but his commitment and empathy gradually begin to break down barriers.

The narrative then explores Thabo's efforts to revitalize community projects that had suffered due to these internal conflicts. He works to reengage members of the community who had withdrawn their participation, emphasizing the importance of collective effort and the shared benefits of successful community initiatives.

Thabo also organizes a series of community-building activities designed to bring people together and foster a spirit of cooperation. These activities include joint community service projects, cultural events, and dialogues. These events provide opportunities for individuals and groups to interact in neutral, positive settings, helping to break down prejudices and build new relationships.

A significant moment in the chapter is a reconciliation ceremony between the feuding families, facilitated by Thabo. This emotionally charged event, attended by many community members, marks a turning point. The families publicly commit to putting their differences aside for the greater good of the community. This act of reconciliation has a powerful impact on the community, setting an example of forgiveness and unity.

As "Mending Broken Bridges" progresses, the positive effects of these reconciliatory efforts become evident. The community starts to heal, and there is a renewed sense of optimism and cooperation. Projects that had been stalled are restarted, and there is a noticeable increase in community engagement and participation.

The chapter concludes with Thabo reflecting on the importance of healing and unity for the long-term health and success of the community. He recognizes that while not all conflicts can be resolved easily, the effort to mend broken bridges is crucial for building a strong, cohesive community.

"Mending Broken Bridges" closes with a community that is more united and resilient, having worked through its differences and conflicts. It's a testament to the power of dialogue, empathy, and the willingness to understand and forgive, essential elements in the journey towards a harmonious and prosperous community.

As "Mending Broken Bridges" continues, Thabo Mokoena's dedication to healing his community's divisions and restoring relationships takes on new dimensions, demonstrating the intricate process of reconciliation and the restoration of trust.

The narrative delves into Thabo's realization that mending relationships extends beyond resolving prominent disputes like the one between the two families. It involves addressing the underlying issues that often lead to misunderstandings and mistrust within the community. Thabo initiates a series of dialogue sessions focused on understanding and addressing these deeper societal issues, such as economic disparities, historical grievances, and cultural misunderstandings.

Thabo also pays special attention to the youth of the community, recognizing that their perspectives and experiences are crucial in shaping a united future. He organizes youth forums where young people can express their views and concerns about the community. These forums prove to be insightful, revealing the younger generation's hopes and apprehensions about their role in the community's future.

A poignant moment in the chapter occurs when Thabo facilitates a meeting between the elders of the community and the youth. This meeting is an opportunity for intergenerational dialogue, where wisdom and experience meet youthful energy and innovation. The session leads to a mutual understanding and a commitment to work together for the community's betterment.

Thabo's efforts to mend broken bridges also lead to the revival of community traditions and celebrations that had fallen by the wayside due to past conflicts. These events become occasions for joy and unity, reinforcing the community's shared heritage and collective identity.

As the chapter progresses, Thabo encourages collaborative community projects that require joint effort from different groups. These projects, ranging from community beautification to the establishment of a local marketplace, serve as practical initiatives for fostering teamwork and mutual respect.

The narrative then shifts to a moment of reflection for Thabo. He walks through the community, observing the renewed sense of camaraderie and witnessing the tangible results of the reconciliation efforts. He sees former adversaries working together, laughter and conversation replacing silence and avoidance.

"Mending Broken Bridges" concludes with a community celebration, marking a year since the initiation of the reconciliation process. This event is a testament to the community's journey, featuring testimonials, cultural performances, and the unveiling of a community mural symbolizing unity and collective strength.

The chapter closes with Thabo addressing the gathering, sharing his thoughts on the power of forgiveness, the strength found in unity, and the importance of continuously working towards harmony and understanding. "Mending Broken Bridges" ends with a reaffirmed sense of community, a collective commitment to ongoing healing and unity, and a recognition of the enduring impact of Thabo's efforts in guiding the community towards a more cohesive and prosperous future.

A VISION REALIZED

A Vision Realized, the narrative culminates in the fulfilment of Thabo Mokoena's long-held dreams and aspirations for his community. This chapter is a celebration of the realization of Thabo's vision, showcasing the transformative impact of his persistent efforts and the community's collective action.

The chapter opens with Thabo overlooking the community from a hilltop, a place where he often came to reflect and dream. He observes the bustling streets, the thriving businesses, the vibrant community centres, and the lush green spaces. It's a scene that closely resembles the vision he had envisioned many years ago – a self-sustaining, united, and prosperous community.

Thabo then takes a walk through the community, interacting with residents and witnessing the fruits of their collective labour. He visits the local schools, now centres of excellence and innovation, and sees children engaged in interactive and creative learning. He stops by the tech incubator, which has become a catalyst for local entrepreneurship and economic development.

One of the highlights of the chapter is the unveiling of a new community project, a state-of-the-art recreational and cultural centre.

This centre, a result of collaborative efforts between the community, local businesses, and government support, symbolizes the harmonious blending of progress and cultural preservation. It offers spaces for arts, sports, education, and community events, serving as a hub for all members of the community.

Thabo also attends a sports event where the soccer team, the pride of the community, plays against a renowned international team. The match is competitive and spirited, reflecting the high level of skill and dedication the team has achieved. The community's support for the team is unwavering, and their success on the international stage is a source of collective pride and joy.

The narrative then shifts to a community assembly, where Thabo is honoured for his contributions. While Thabo appreciates the recognition, he redirects the accolades to the community members, emphasizing that the realization of the vision was a collective achievement. He speaks about the power of community, the importance of shared dreams, and the need for continued effort to sustain and build upon their achievements.

As "A Vision Realized" draws to a close, Thabo reflects on his journey. He thinks about the challenges, the setbacks, and the victories. He realizes that while his initial vision has been realized, the community's journey does not end here. It's an ongoing process of growth, adaptation, and improvement.

The chapter concludes with a community celebration, a festive and joyful event that brings together all members of the community. It's a reflection of the unity, strength, and vibrancy of the community – a living embodiment of Thabo's vision realized.

"A Vision Realized" closes with a sense of accomplishment and a forward-looking optimism. It's a testament to the enduring power of a shared vision and the remarkable transformation that can occur when a community comes together to turn dreams into reality.

As "A Vision Realized" progresses, Thabo Mokoena's reflective journey through the community he has helped to transform continues, deepening the sense of fulfilment and anticipation for the future.

Thabo visits a community garden project, a green oasis that was once a neglected and barren plot of land. This garden is not only a source of fresh produce for the community but also a place of learning and gathering, promoting environmental awareness and healthy living. Thabo meets with the volunteers who maintain the garden, exchanging stories and ideas. This project, born from a simple idea, has grown into a vital part of the community's life.

Next, Thabo stops by a new small business incubator, an offshoot of the original tech incubator, now focused on a broader range of entrepreneurial ventures.

He sees a diverse group of entrepreneurs working on various projects, from artisan crafts to innovative tech solutions. The energy and creativity in the space are palpable, and Thabo feels a surge of pride in the enterprising spirit of his community.

The narrative then takes Thabo to a local healthcare centre, which has evolved significantly. It now offers not just basic medical services but also wellness programs and preventative care, contributing to the overall well-being of the community. Thabo speaks with healthcare workers and patients, witnessing the positive impacts of accessible and quality healthcare.

As Thabo continues his walk, he encounters various community members – from young students who aspire to be leaders to elders who have witnessed the transformation of their community over the years. Each interaction is a reminder of the interconnectedness of the community and the collective effort that has fuelled its growth.

The chapter reaches an emotional peak when Thabo revisits the soccer field where it all began. He watches a group of children playing, coached by some of the original team members who have now become mentors themselves. This scene symbolizes the cycle of mentorship and community development that Thabo has always championed.

In the final scenes of "A Vision Realized," Thabo attends a community forum where residents discuss future projects and initiatives. The forum demonstrates the proactive and engaged nature of the community, always looking forward to new ways to improve and develop. Thabo listens more than he speaks, his role now more of an advisor and elder statesman.

The chapter concludes with Thabo giving a short speech at the forum. He talks about the journey they have all been on, the importance of continuing to dream and strive for improvement, and the need to nurture and pass on the values of community, collaboration, and resilience to future generations.

"A Vision Realized" closes with a community that is not just transformed but also energized and forward-looking. It's a testament to Thabo's vision and the collective will of a community that dared to dream and worked tirelessly to make those dreams a reality. The story ends with a sense of closure for Thabo's direct involvement but an open door for the ongoing evolution of the vibrant community he has helped to shape.

THE POWER OF UNITY

The Power of Unity, the focus shifts to the collective strength and solidarity of Thabo Mokoena's community, highlighting how unity has been the cornerstone of their success and resilience. This chapter is a celebration of the community's spirit of togetherness and the collaborative efforts that have led to substantial and lasting change.

The chapter opens with the community facing a new challenge, a proposed development project by external investors that threatens to disrupt the community's harmony and way of life. This situation tests the community's unity and the strength of the relationships and networks that Thabo and others have built over the years.

Thabo, playing a more advisory role, watches as community leaders and members come together to discuss and address this challenge. There are differences in opinions and approaches, but the underlying commitment to the community's well-being is evident. The community's ability to engage in open, constructive dialogue is a testament to the culture of unity and mutual respect that has been cultivated.

The narrative then shifts to a series of community meetings and workshops organized to formulate a response to the development project.

These meetings are inclusive, with representatives from different sectors of the community, including youth, elders, business owners, and local activists. The discussions are robust, and through these collaborative efforts, the community develops a unified strategy to address the issue.

Thabo's role in these meetings is subtle yet impactful. He shares his insights and experiences, guiding the discussions without dominating them. His emphasis on unity and collective decision-making resonates with the community members, reminding them of the strength they possess when they work together.

A significant moment in the chapter is when the community presents a united front in negotiations with the investors. They articulate their concerns and propose alternatives that align with the community's values and needs. This unified approach leads to a favourable outcome, where the development project is adjusted to benefit both the investors and the community.

The narrative also explores the broader implications of the community's unity. This incident becomes a rallying point, strengthening the community's sense of identity and purpose. It inspires other initiatives, such as community-led development projects and collaborative ventures that leverage the collective skills and resources of the community members.

As "The Power of Unity" concludes, the community celebrates their victory over the development project. This celebration is more than just a recognition of the successful outcome; it's a recognition of the community's ability to come together and advocate for its interests.

The chapter closes with Thabo reflecting on the journey of the community. He realizes that the true power of the community lies in its unity – the ability to come together in times of need, to respect and value diverse perspectives, and to work collaboratively towards common goals. "The Power of Unity" ends with a sense of hope and confidence in the community's future, a future that is built on the solid foundation of unity and togetherness.

As "The Power of Unity" progresses, the narrative delves deeper into the enduring strength and cohesiveness of Thabo Mokoena's community, illustrating how their collective spirit and solidarity have become the bedrock for facing challenges and fostering growth.

Following the community's triumph in the negotiations with the investors, there is a renewed sense of empowerment among the community members. This victory reinforces their belief in the power of unity and collective action. It becomes a catalyst for further collaborative efforts and initiatives aimed at enhancing the community's well-being.

Thabo, observing these developments, feels a profound sense of pride. He had always envisioned a community where unity was not just a concept but a lived reality. Now, he sees this vision manifesting in tangible ways. The community's ability to unite and act cohesively under pressure is a testament to the strength of the bonds formed over the years.

The narrative then shifts to highlight several community-driven projects that have stemmed from this renewed sense of unity. One such project is a community-led environmental initiative that brings together people of all ages to work on urban greening and sustainability. This project not only improves the community's environment but also strengthens communal ties as people work side by side for a common cause.

Another significant development is the formation of a community council, representing various groups within the community. This council becomes a platform for discussing and addressing local issues, ensuring that all voices are heard and considered in decision-making processes. Thabo plays a role in mentoring the council members, emphasizing the importance of inclusive and transparent governance.

Thabo also witnesses how the unity within the community begins to influence and inspire neighbouring communities and regions. The success story of Thabo's community, particularly their approach to handling the development project, becomes a model for others. Delegations from other communities visit to learn and exchange ideas, creating a network of communities united by shared values and goals.

As "The Power of Unity" nears its conclusion, the community organizes a cultural festival that celebrates their diversity and unity. The festival features music, dance, art, and food from various cultures represented in the community, showcasing the richness of their collective heritage. Thabo looks on as people from different backgrounds come together in celebration, a living embodiment of the unity he has always championed.

The chapter concludes with a reflective Thabo addressing the festival attendees. He speaks about the journey they have undertaken together, the obstacles they have overcome, and the power of standing united in the face of adversity. He reminds them that while they have achieved much, the journey of maintaining and nurturing their unity is ongoing.

"The Power of Unity" closes with a community that is not just stronger but also more aware of its collective power. It's a testament to the idea that unity, in all its forms, is one of the greatest strengths a community can possess. The story ends with a message of hope and a call to continue fostering the spirit of togetherness for future generations.

FINAL REDEMPTION

Final Redemption, the narrative brings Thabo Mokoena's journey full circle, focusing on a pivotal moment that signifies the culmination of his efforts and the healing of old wounds. This chapter is a poignant reflection on redemption, both for Thabo personally and for the community he has devoted his life to.

The chapter begins with an unexpected development. A figure from Thabo's past, a person with whom he had a significant conflict during the early years of his community work, returns to the community. This individual, once a source of contention and strife, has come back to make amends, seeking forgiveness and reconciliation.

Thabo is initially taken aback by this unexpected reunion. Memories of past conflicts resurface, reminding him of the challenging periods he navigated in his quest to uplift the community. However, he sees this as an opportunity for closure and healing, not just for himself but for the community as well.

The narrative then follows Thabo as he engages in a series of conversations with this individual. These discussions are deeply introspective, allowing both parties to express their perspectives, regrets, and hopes for the future. This process is not easy, but it's marked by a sense of maturity and the desire to move forward.

Parallel to this personal reconciliation, the chapter explores the theme of redemption within the community. Thabo witnesses the transformation of individuals and groups who were once on opposing sides of community issues. He sees former adversaries collaborating on projects, contributing to the community's growth, and building new relationships based on mutual respect and understanding.

A significant moment in the chapter is a community gathering organized to celebrate the spirit of reconciliation and redemption. This event becomes a platform for sharing stories of transformation, forgiveness, and renewed collaboration. Thabo, along with the individual from his past, addresses the gathering, sharing their journey of reconciliation as an example of the power of forgiveness and the possibility of change.

As "Final Redemption" draws to a close, Thabo reflects on the journey he has undertaken. He realizes that redemption is not a single act but a continuous process of learning, growing, and healing. He feels a sense of peace and fulfilment, knowing that his efforts have contributed to creating a community where redemption and second chances are possible.

The community, having embraced the principles of forgiveness and reconciliation, stands as a testament to the idea that redemption is achievable, no matter how difficult the past.

"Final Redemption" closes with a message of enduring optimism and the belief that it's never too late to make amends and build a better future.

As "Final Redemption" continues, the deepening of Thabo Mokoena's and the community's journey into forgiveness and healing further reinforces the transformative power of redemption and reconciliation. The chapter delves into how Thabo's personal reconciliation with his former adversary becomes a catalyst for broader healing within the community.

This reconciliation is not merely symbolic; it initiates a series of dialogues and peace-building activities. Thabo uses this experience to teach and inspire others about the importance of confronting past grievances to build a more harmonious future.

A pivotal development in the chapter is the establishment of a community reconciliation initiative. This program, inspired by Thabo's experience, is designed to help others resolve long-standing conflicts and differences. It includes workshops, mediation sessions, and communal events, all aimed at fostering a culture of understanding and forgiveness. Thabo, while not leading, remains a key figure in guiding and supporting this initiative.

Thabo also takes this time to reconnect with various individuals who have been part of his journey – old friends, former rivals, and colleagues.

These reunions are emotional and reflective, filled with shared memories and new understandings. They serve to close old chapters and strengthen the bonds that have been formed over the years.

The narrative then shifts to a powerful community event, where stories of redemption and reconciliation are shared. Individuals who have gone through the reconciliation initiative speak about their experiences, sharing their journeys from conflict to understanding. This event becomes a profound testament to the community's capacity for change and growth.

As "Final Redemption" nears its conclusion, Thabo reflects on his role in shaping the community. He realizes that his greatest contribution has been in empowering others to lead and fostering a community where redemption and healing are possible. He sees a community that is not only thriving but also compassionate and resilient.

The chapter concludes with a touching scene where Thabo revisits the hilltop where he used to envision the future of the community. As he looks out over the transformed landscape, he feels a profound sense of contentment and hope.

The community he dreamed of is now a reality – a place of unity, growth, and second chances. "Final Redemption" closes with the community moving forward, guided by the lessons of the past and the promise of a better future. It's a testament to the enduring power of forgiveness and the human capacity for renewal and change. The story ends with a message of optimism, celebrating the journey of a community that has found strength and unity in its ability to heal and redeem itself.

LEGACY OF A LEADER

Legacy of a Leader, the story comes to a poignant culmination, focusing on Thabo Mokoena's enduring legacy within the community. This chapter is a reflective and inspiring look at the lasting impact Thabo has made, not only through his initiatives but also through the values and principles he has instilled in the community.

The chapter begins with the community preparing to honour Thabo for his decades of service and dedication. While Thabo is initially reluctant to be the centre of attention, he eventually understands that this celebration is as much for the community as it is for him. It's a moment for everyone to reflect on their journey and the progress they have made together.

As the community gathers for the event, there is a sense of deep gratitude and respect for Thabo. Various members of the community come forward to share their stories and experiences, highlighting how Thabo's leadership and mentorship have touched their lives. These testimonies range from young entrepreneurs who were inspired by Thabo's tech incubator to families who benefited from the community programs he initiated.

The narrative then explores the tangible aspects of Thabo's legacy. The thriving community centre, the successful soccer team, the innovative tech incubator, and the vibrant community gardens are all enduring testaments to his vision and effort. However, Thabo's most significant legacy is seen in the intangible – the sense of unity, resilience, and empowerment that pervades the community.

Thabo's influence extends beyond the projects he spearheaded. His approach to leadership – emphasizing empathy, collaboration, and ethical conduct – has become a model for current and future leaders in the community. Thabo's philosophy of empowering others to lead has ensured that the community's progress and initiatives are sustainable.

As the event progresses, a surprise announcement is made. The community reveals plan to establish a leadership and development institute in Thabo's name. This institute is envisioned as a space to nurture future generations of community leaders, guided by the principles and values that Thabo has championed. He speaks with humility and wisdom, reflecting on the importance of community, the power of collective effort, and the need to continuously strive for improvement and growth. He expresses his gratitude and shares his hope that the community will continue to thrive and be a beacon of positive change.

"Legacy of a Leader" is a sense of completion and continuity. Thabo's journey may have reached a turning point, but his legacy lives on in the hearts and actions of the community he helped shape. The chapter ends with a message of enduring hope and inspiration, celebrating the journey of a leader whose impact will be felt for generations to come.

As "Legacy of a Leader" unfolds, the depth and breadth of Thabo Mokoena's impact on the community become even more evident, painting a rich portrait of a leader whose influence has deeply ingrained itself into the fabric of the community.

The narrative shifts to focus on individual stories within the community, each a testament to Thabo's influence. A young woman speaks about how Thabo's mentorship helped her launch a social enterprise that now provides employment to many in the community. A former athlete from the soccer team, inspired by Thabo's emphasis on education, shares his journey of becoming a teacher who is now shaping young minds.

The establishment of the Thabo Mokoena Leadership and Development Institute takes centre stage in the chapter. Thabo is deeply moved by this gesture, seeing it as a continuation of his life's work. The institute is designed to offer leadership training, community development programs, and entrepreneurship workshops, embodying Thabo's holistic approach to community empowerment.

Thabo's personal reflections provide a poignant backdrop to the chapter. He reminisces about the early days of his work, the challenges faced, and the milestones achieved. Thabo acknowledges that while his journey had its share of obstacles, every step was worth the sense of accomplishment he feels seeing the community's transformation.

The narrative then explores how Thabo's legacy extends beyond specific projects or initiatives. His greatest legacy is in the mindset and culture he has helped cultivate in the community – a culture of resilience, mutual support, collaboration, and continuous learning. Thabo's principles of leadership have inspired a generation of community members to lead with integrity, compassion, and a commitment to the greater good.

As the chapter nears its end, a celebration is held in the community square. This event is not just in honour of Thabo but also a celebration of the community's journey and achievements. Music, dance, and laughter fill the air, symbolizing the joy and unity that have become hallmarks of the community.

"Legacy of a Leader" concludes with Thabo taking a moment to address the community. He speaks not of farewells but of new beginnings, encouraging the community to continue building on the foundations laid. He talks about the endless possibilities that lie ahead and the importance of passing on the legacy of community service and leadership to future generations.

The chapter closes with a sense of fulfilment and hope. Thabo's journey may have reached a milestone, but his legacy continues to thrive in the community he loves. "Legacy of a Leader" ends as a tribute to the enduring impact of a visionary leader and the collective power of a community united in purpose and action.

EPILOGUE: FIRST THE PEOPLE, THEN THE MONEY WILL FOLLOW

In the epilogue, "First the People, Then the Money will follow" the story of Thabo Mokoena and his community comes to a reflective and inspiring conclusion. This final section encapsulates Thabo's guiding philosophy that prioritizing people and their well-being leads to true and lasting prosperity.

The epilogue opens with Thabo in a quieter, more contemplative phase of his life. He spends his days engaged in various community activities, but now more as a mentor and elder statesman than as a frontline leader. His days are filled with conversations with young leaders, casual visits to various community projects, and time spent in reflection.

Thabo's philosophy of "First the People, Then the Money will follow" has become a guiding principle for the community. This approach, focusing on the well-being and empowerment of individuals as the foundation for economic growth and development, has led to a thriving community where economic success is balanced with social responsibility.

The narrative highlights how this philosophy has transformed the community's approach to business and development. Local enterprises and initiatives prioritize sustainable practices, community engagement, and ethical operations.

The success of these enterprises has attracted attention from other communities and regions, turning Thabo's community into a model for holistic and sustainable development.

The epilogue also explores the broader impact of Thabo's work. His influence has extended beyond the community, inspiring change in neighbouring areas and even at regional policy levels. The principles he championed – community involvement, ethical leadership, and sustainable development – are now part of larger conversations about social and economic progress.

As the epilogue draws to a close, Thabo reflects on his journey and the evolution of his community. He feels a profound sense of satisfaction, seeing the values he has always believed in come to fruition. He realizes that true wealth is not just in financial prosperity but in the health, happiness, and unity of the community.

"First the People, Then the Money will follow" concludes with a community event where Thabo is asked to speak. He shares his insights on the importance of putting people first, the interconnectedness of community and individual well-being, and the long-term benefits of sustainable development. His speech is met with applause and admiration, a testament to the respect and love the community holds for him.

The epilogue ends with Thabo watching a sunset from his favourite hilltop, reflecting on the journey that has been and the future that lies ahead. He is content, knowing that the community is in capable hands and that his legacy will continue to guide it. "First the People, Then the Money will follow" closes not just as the end of Thabo's story but as a beginning for the community and its ongoing journey towards a future where people and their well-being are at the heart of progress and prosperity.

AFTERWORD BY ONESIMUS MALATJI: THE AUTHOR AND CREATIVE BUSINESSMAN

In the afterword, Onesimus Malatji, the author and creative businessman, provides personal insights and reflections on the creation of this narrative. This section serves as a bridge between the story of Thabo Mokoena and the real-world experiences and philosophies of Malatji himself.

Onesimus Malatji begins by sharing the inspiration behind the story of Thabo Mokoena. Drawing from his own experiences as a creative businessman and his observations of community dynamics, Malatji crafted Thabo's character and journey to encapsulate the challenges, triumphs, and complexities of leading social and economic change in a community.

Malatji discusses the central theme of the narrative – the concept of "First the People, Then the Money will follow." He explains how this principle has guided his own approach to business and community development. For Malatji, the well-being and empowerment of people are paramount, and true success, both in business and in community building, stems from prioritizing human values and needs.

The afterword delves into Malatji's reflections on leadership and community empowerment. He shares his belief in the power of mentorship, collaboration, and ethical leadership – themes that are vividly portrayed in Thabo's story. Malatji emphasizes the importance of nurturing future generations of leaders who are equipped to tackle social and economic challenges with empathy, integrity, and innovation.

Malatji also addresses the challenges of writing this story, particularly the task of weaving together the various strands of community life, business, and personal growth into a coherent and inspiring narrative. He speaks about his creative process and how his experiences and observations have shaped the development of the characters and the plot.

In discussing the impact, he hopes the story will have, Malatji expresses his desire for readers to find inspiration and insight in Thabo's journey. He hopes that the story will spark discussions about sustainable development, social responsibility, and the role of leadership in creating positive change.

The afterword concludes with Malatji expressing his gratitude to the readers and his hope that the story of Thabo Mokoena will resonate with them, encouraging reflection, action, and a commitment to making a difference in their communities and spheres of influence.

Onesimus Malatji signs off with a message of optimism and encouragement, reiterating his belief in the potential of individuals and communities to drive meaningful change when guided by the principles of unity, empathy, and a steadfast focus on the well-being of people.

~~~~~~~~~~~~~~~~~END~~~~~~~~~~~~~~~~~~

www.ingramcontent.com/pod-product-compliance
Lightning Source LLC
Chambersburg PA
CBHW021101080526
44587CB00010B/335